THE TIME GATHERER

Patrick Pye

THE
TIME GATHERER

A study of El Greco's
treatment of the sacred theme

FOUR COURTS PRESS, DUBLIN

The typesetting for this book
was produced by Seton Music Graphics Ltd for
Four Courts Press Ltd,
Kill Lane, Blackrock, Co. Dublin.

A CIP record for this title
is available from the British Library.

ISBN 1 85182 084 1

Printed in England by
Abacus Colour Printers Ltd, Lowick,
and Billing and Son Ltd, Worcester

CONTENTS

LIST OF ILLUSTRATIONS   7

ACKNOWLEDGMENTS   9

I
The Enigma   11

II
Byzantine Crete and Domenikos Theotokopolous   17

III
The Gentleman Artist abroad   24

IV
The Paintings   33

V
Mannerist Times and the Platonic Inhibition   56

VI
A Visionary Art within the Church   73

VII
In Praise of Solitude   96

VIII
The Time Gatherer   103

APPENDIX:
A Sufi Definition of Imagination   119

NOTES   123

ILLUSTRATIONS

(by El Greco, unless otherwise stated)

COLOUR PLATES   *between pages* 32 *and* 33

1   *The Assumption*

2   *The Arrest of Christ*

3   *The Two Ss. John*

4   *The Crucifixion*

5   *The Resurrection*

6   *Laocoön*

7   School of Novgorod (15th century), *Pentecost*

8   *Pentecost*

BLACK AND WHITE

1   Boy Lighting a Candle   25

2   Adoration of the Holy Name   29

3   The Holy Trinity   35

4   Karl Schmidt-Rottluf, *Christ and the Adulteress*, 1918   67

5   Raphael, The Sistine Madonna   69

6   Burial of Count Orgaz   77

7   The Resurrection of the Elect   91

8   Christ Healing the Blind Man   107

ACKNOWLEDGMENTS

For the following pages I am deeply indebted in a personal way to Fr Paul Murray OP, whose patient and careful midwifery of this text were my main encouragement, and to my wife, Noirin, wonderfully letting me be so absorbed.

I am also indebted to Mr Richard Wood, to Fr Philip McShane OP, to Aosdána, to the Tyrone Guthrie Centre at Annaghmakerrig, to Richard Weber, Librarian, National College of Art and Design, and to my old friends on whose patience I drew for making this work possible.

The works reproduced in this book appear by kind permission of (for figures): fig. 1 Galleria Nazionale di Capodimonti, Naples; fig. 2 Patrimonio Nacional, Madrid; fig. 3 Museo del Prado, Madrid; fig. 5 Staatliche Kunstsammlungen Dresden; fig. 6 Don Fernando Hilario Pinel, párroco, Parroquía de Santo Tomás, Toledo; fig. 7 Metropolitan Museum of Art (New York), Rogers Fund, 1956; fig. 8 Galleria Nazionale, Parma; and (for colour plates): pl. 1 Courtesy of The Art Institute of Chicago; pl. 2 Ilmo. Sr. Deán de la Catedral de Toledo; pl. 3 Museo de Santa Cruz, Toledo; pls. 4, 5 and 8 Museo Nacional del Prado, Madrid; pl. 6 National Gallery of Art, Washington, Samuel H. Kress Collection; pl. 7 SVS Press, Crestwood, New York's edition of Ouspensky and Lossky's *The Meaning of Icons*.

I

THE ENIGMA

When I turned to the only adjacent sympathetic adult available to me to share my discovery of the extraordinary paintings of El Greco, I was warned. My mother—my confidant of the time—received the news of my conversion coolly. It was, perhaps, precipitous of one who was only sixteen to talk of his life being 'changed', but I was not to be put off. 'I know,' said my mother, 'El Greco does seem to do that to people, but I wouldn't take it too seriously.' Then she told me about the musical editor of the Oxford University Press with whom she had worked in her unmarried days. He was a brilliant if effervescent man called Mr Foss, a man who was celebrated for the wild and hilarious games that he invented to play with his children. He had left the office for lunch one day perfectly normal, and had come back three hours later like a lunatic. He had just seen the *Christ driving the Traders out of the Temple* by El Greco in the London National Gallery and he too had stridden up and down the office in front of my mother saying how his ' . . . life would never be the same.' She did not wholly dismiss El Greco because of the man he had affected so cathartically, but for her son's benefit she sounded a strong note of caution.

I was not to be shaken. Already in the forties art reproduction had wrought a new plurality of taste, and I had begun to pay attention to certain modern masters working both sides of 1900. They encouraged me to see form in a more musical and abstract way than the descriptive naturalism encouraged by the academies. I had quietly imbibed a whole new sensibility, and in El Greco I found an old master who corroborated this. My mother was musical, I allowed, but I could see that when she looked at paintings her music was left on some remote shelf.

I partook, furthermore, of the rediscovery of William Blake that affected so many on these islands at the end of the war. It was his philosophical epigrams and poems that occupied me most. His description of the function of imagination for the artist was, for me, definitive. Alas, then, that I could not conceal from myself a disappointment with his practice as a painter. The sources for the bricks and mortar of his style were just too evident to convince me that imagination had always been allowed to complete its labour. With El Greco I felt no such qualms. Here was a painter who practised perfectly what Blake preached. Here was a totally self-sufficient world of the imagination, conceived in the consistency of a fine intelligence, with incomparably bold execution.

I saw my limitation before such an achievement, but nothing mitigated for me the discovery that painting could, apparently, augur the life of God within us. The perspective of the marvellous opened up by that revelation has never deserted me.

Perhaps the 'marvellous' is not considered a serious perspective in the West. Marvels are for children who experience life as a gift along with their mother's care and their father's providing. The serious business in life is the exploration of the oyster that is given to us—the world. For a few hundred years now the West has been under the cloud of this exploration. At first the exploration did not involve us in serious impiety for God was seen to be reflected in his creation. Surreptitiously, however, in taking upon ourselves the role of explorer, in pursuing the tasting of the world at the behest of our own will, we made ourselves Gods. We forgot that the oyster was a gift. The more entangled we became in this exploration the more we forgot that we were part of the oyster—the creation of an original Creator. We are vulnerable. We reap what we sow. In making over the world we have lost a most precious sense—the sense of ourselves as creatures along with, rather than up against, the rest of creation.

I do not think I need to labour the point. Our subjection of the world has turned it into a prison. The built world becomes a mirror where man sees only himself. The loss of our creaturely sense has brought such misery and unhappiness upon us, that it may indeed be time to think seriously about the marvellous again. As the man said, 'Explanation we have in plenty: now what we need is inspiration!'

My reaction as a teenage youth turning the pages of an art book in the school library was, you could say, emotional and spontaneous. The business of settling into life (what adults call the real business of life) is a slow process of coming to terms with limitation. What happier escape, then, for reluctant youth than into the pages of an art book on El Greco—especially, it must be said, when the paintings contemplated bear so little relation to the world outside, whose limits must be accepted. I readily admit the measure of escape in this turning of the pages. I insist, though, on the innocence of this escape. It was from the space given me by this escape that I came to accept the limitations we must all encounter with (some) grace and sense of their meaning. There was no listless dreaminess in my attentions to El Greco. This was not due to my own spotlessness, but to the purity of the artist's vision: there is no pandering to subjective fantasy in El Greco's images. They offer no wish-fulfilment to the ego of the one who contemplates them. The wonder that they call upon in our souls is pure of selfhood.

At the time I did not really understand what El Greco's art was about. My understanding of Catholicism (to which my parents did not subscribe) was rudimentary. To me his work seemed mystical. If the art of the Middle Ages appeared to me to be an objective, ecclesial art, El Greco's appeared as a sort of art of the Christian experience, an art of our inner life. If someone described his work to me as 'romantic', I would have been the last to disallow that description. I would have recognized, though, how different it is from what passes as Romanticism in the histories of art.

Theology is, among other things, a study of the structure of the marvellous. The Church often forgets this in its struggle to make its case plausible in a materialist culture. What is more marvellous than God's love for us? It is only our wonder at this marvel, our permission of this wonder in the depths of our hearts, that gives the intellect a warrant for the activity of theologizing at all. Nothing is more radical than the presence or absence of God. The traditional position of the Church is that, in all our capacity for knowing, it is only in the wisdom of the Church that our knowledge has objectivity. What we know of the world is never quite separate from what we are as creatures in it. In the becoming of the world the being of God is the only fact that really deserves the title of 'objectivity'.

El Greco's painting is really part of a great theological enterprise, the enterprise of Tridentine theology. That we have been so slow to see this is largely because we in the twentieth century have grown so far from our Christian and Classical roots. The rediscovery of El Greco did not come from Christians, but from the Romantics, the last people who tried to hold sense and sensibility together. Then he was discovered by the Post-impressionists, who were trying to create a new visual language. They saw in him the Old Master who had the greatest sensitivity to real problems of formal language as the artist understands them. It remains for our generation to place him squarely in the tradition of European Christian art.

The difficulty of placing his work in the centre is that the circumference is so manifestly different. To anyone brought up on the painting from Raphael to Velazquez it is hard to see beyond the distinctiveness of El Greco's style. To eyes that are aculturised by that period (as our great grandfathers' were) it is hard to see beyond the elongation of the form and the bravura brushwork. The will behind the form escapes them; why the artist painted some parts quite representationally and other parts abstractly, why so many of his works are divided so radically between the heavenly and earthly regions: these things escape their comprehension. They can only see a wilfully flaunted anti-naturalism and their acknowledgement of it does not exceed a Mannerist essay in a decorative style. They may indeed sense a religious content in the work, but so extreme to them seem the means sought to convey this content that they are very loath to allow it.

Time passes and things appear in a new light. Very few acquainted with the heritage of painting now are limited to the couple of hundred years between Raphael and Velazquez. The so-called 'Primitives', from being regarded by our great-grandparents as gauche antecedents of the achievements of the High Renaissance, are now taken seriously as masters in their own right. The scales of a certain prejudice have fallen from our eyes.

But these prejudices are remarkably complex things, obdurate to penetration. No doubt they were begat by previous prejudices. We can only work to uncover them slowly, piece by piece. And the surprises that greet us sometimes confound our own prejudices and sometimes mystify us.

Since the first rediscovery of El Greco by the Romantics much study has been done of the Toledo of which he was an eminent citizen. The Romantics had placed him firmly among their lonely tormented selves. Study reveals that no maverick artist was he, but a friend of canon lawyers, poets, novelists and theologians, esteemed at the centre of the society he belonged to. It is accepted now that he acted on a commission for the renewal of art in the Church according to the strict rules laid down by the Council of Trent. His style does not seem to have presented a problem to his own generation. Certain iconographic liberties in his paintings caused his contemporaries to balk, but we hear nothing of the so-called 'excesses' of his style till fifty or sixty years after his death. What was the shift in communal apprehension that allowed his own generation to accept so radical a style as normal and appropriate for religious or ecclesiastical usage, and deprived their successors of the same acceptance?

When I left school, El Greco continued to occupy a prime place in my firmament. However, I realised that the peculiar brilliance of his work made him dangerous to emulate, and my main attentions became divided between the Medievals and certain contemporary artists. When I visited Spain in my twenties I did notice that Spaniards constantly referred to him as 'un pintor clásico'. That surprised me rather, but it was not until much later when I received a beautifully produced compendium of his work that I suddenly saw how classical his painting was. The quest for the real El Greco has occupied me ever since.

This short book, then, is not a life of the artist. It is not, properly speaking, a critical study of the body of his work. It is purely speculation, and nothing will be definitely proved by the end of it. In justification of such an exercise I can only say that El Greco saw his own work as a similar speculation, an activity of the intuitive intellect at the boundaries between the knowable and the unknowable, between the seen and the unseen. All over the world 'hommes moyen sensuels' are struck in wonder at the peculiar boldness of El Greco's 'speculation'. I only claim that such a wonder is worth examining—I, 'un homme moyen sensuel' among others.

'What is truth?' That is the supremely worldly question that has all our subjectivities hopping anxiously. Allow, on the other hand, that truth is esoteric, that it belongs to the 'mysterium' in which we all partake, and immediately the grip-hold of subjectivity is loosened. My individual relationship to 'truth' becomes, then, rather than one of claim, one of studentship and apprenticeship.

Long ago I found I only had to come down on one side or the other on a certain matter—whether the scandal of Christ's incarnation and crucifixion is a historical scandal, or whether it is a scandal that sits enthroned at the very heart of existence. Of course, I cannot weigh up so extraordinary a matter, any more, I imagine, than Domenikos Theotokopolous could. An answer chooses me, and I, very weakly, say 'yes' to it.

II

BYZANTINE CRETE AND
DOMENIKOS THEOTOKOPOLOUS

The Crete where El Greco was christened Domenikos Theotokopolous in 1541 (his Spanish name being a mere appellation) was no provincial backwater. A strategic trading post in the eastern Mediterranean, it was a centre of Orthodox Christianity ruled from Catholic and cosmopolitan Venice. When the Eastern Empire finally collapsed before the Turks in 1453, many studios of icon painters moved from Constantinople to Candia, with the result that Crete became home to the last flowering of Byzantine culture. Whether the young Domenikos' family were part of the Venetian administration we do not know, but they were Catholic and the boy was received of the classical and literary education favoured by the well-to-do of the time.

Since by this time the Catholic minority on the island was sizeable and influential enough, some studios were well into the habit of painting in the 'Greek' style for the Orthodox while supplying the Catholic community with work understood to be in the 'Italian' style. The Greek style having its roots deepest in the island, it is not, perhaps, surprising to find that the Western style was a rather weak derivation from certain late-Gothic schools on mainland Italy. The Greek style had the sophistication of a true continuity, while the Western style was imported (under some misapprehensions), having little to do with the ferment of innovation that now possessed its homeland. Tradition allows us to assume some interchange between these two major groupings of picture production as the better studios were not just working for the home market, but were exporting icons to Italy and Germany. Already art-conscious princes and gentlemen were adopting the fashion of making collections and a brisk trade in icons developed from Crete as far north as Cologne and the Baltic Sea. Sizeable

Catholic and Orthodox communities from Crete in Venice itself employed the artists of the island for their needs.

In the hundred years coming up to El Greco's birth Crete shared in a special destiny. Heir to the greatest of the impersonal theosophical art styles of the Middle Ages through its vassalage to Venice, it became just that melting pot that may have made El Greco's art possible. In the local studio situation as he found it El Greco functioned very ably until his mid twenties. In his pilgrimage westwards (and may it not have been more a 'seeking' than an exile?) he later personalised the style of his antecedents, discreetly and in accordance with some new religious perceptions, but the sacred nature of his assumptions remained at the core of his own art. Those we must now examine.

At the centre of everything in Byzantine society was the Word that the Father had uttered in his Son, the Christ. From the prestige of this 'word' came the prestige of every other word. Utterance had a weight and reverberation that are hard for us to appreciate today. In the rudimentary domestic technology of the time the word rang out with a bell-like sonority. For Byzantine man words were no less than his first technique, the way the world was identified from its primal causes. For us, words live on the surface. They change meaning several times in a generation and it is hard for us to say, even with so recent a figure as W.B. Yeats that '. . . words alone are certain good'. For Byzantine man words were Promethean fire. He was too near word's primal function of 'naming' not to see the solemnity of such a cypher. By 'naming' man continued God's creation, and each time he 'named' the appropriate image was born in his heart that answered the name.

The beginning of everything is in mystery, in the original wonder and gift of being, and in the stories in which God's freedom is exemplified for us. The origin of every work of art is in myth, but what the myth initiates is by no means simple. Word and its reverberation, image, contain their mutual incompatibility within their simplicity. Even today children learn to indicate the identity of each created being with a circle, and that simplicity supersedes all further definitions. The unremitting logic of this history of origins unfolds the bond of image and word in the hands of priests. The priests were custodians of the word, but since the image is only the inference of the word in the heart it should not surprise us to find that 'iconography'—as is properly called the painting of icons—developed first as a discipline of contemplation allowed to some of the brethren in a monastic community.

Of all the stretches of time into which European history has fallen, that of the Eastern Empire was the longest and most homogeneous. El Greco's life was contiguous to this long period and its essential Christian structure he irrevocably absorbed. Our trouble today in appreciating a different sort of past is that, as a historically conscious culture, we need the distractions of history: an a historical culture is almost inconceivable to us.

For Byzantium the Crucifixion fixed history. Before this event the Judaic ban on sacred imagery kept the mind in a darkness and potentiality of knowing; with it a destiny is consummated, a darkness is penetrated and an 'image' is given to the world, the image, no less, of the Father given in the Son. The basis of icon painting is this—that we, in making an image of the Son, continue God's creation after the unique pattern that the Father has provided for us. We see this working itself out through the conflict between the Iconoclasts and the Iconodules when finally the Church is able to announce that

> certain holy icons have the image of a lamb, at which is pointing the finger of the Forerunner. This lamb is taken as the image of grace, representing the true Lamb, Christ our God, whom the law foreshadowed. Thus accepting with love the ancient images and shadows as prefigurations and symbols of truth transmitted to the Church, we prefer grace and truth, receiving it as the fulfilment of the law. Thus in order to make plain this fulfilment for all to see, if only by means of pictures, we ordain that from henceforth icons should represent, instead of the lamb of old, the human image of the Lamb, Who has taken upon himself the sins of the world, Christ our God. . . . (Trullan Council, 691 A.D.)

Defending the icon the Church was not just defending its educational role, much less its aesthetic value: it saw itself defending the very foundations of Christian faith, the visible testimony of God made man as the basis of our salvation.

Iconography required of its practitioners a rigorous spiritual discipline to prepare the artist (as such he was) and develop his sensitivity to the layers of correspondences implicit in his theme.

Scripture, like life itself, was seen as an onion to be read on at least three levels of skin—the literal, the analogical and the spiritual. A proper interpretation of Scripture was one in which the reading at each level was both consistent in itself, and without contradiction in relation to the levels of meaning below and above it. Inspiring and enriching these layers were the respective roles played by the Old and New Testaments—the prophetic role of the one and the fulfilling role of the other. Further were the cosmological and metaphysical readings which the Church had taken over from Greek thought as tools of its own explication.

Man, created in the image and likeness of God, had, then, the Divine Word for archetype. That is why the incarnation of the Son renews the image which had lost its 'likeness' through the sin of Adam. What, then, is the guiding principle for the icon-ographer in attaining the 'likeness' of Christ? If Christ, the 'last Adam', showed himself as the archetype of the 'first man', in the abasement of his redemptive work he now takes on the likeness of fallen human nature, which is an 'unlikeness' belonging to the aspect of the 'Servant', of the 'Man of Sorrows'. Christ is seen to unite two aspects of 'likeness' in his earthly life—that of his glorious likeness and that of his kenotic unlikeness—'form of God' with 'form of Servant', the former being dissimulated by the latter for outward eyes. Hence the great significance for the icon-ographers of the disciples' difficulty in recognising the Risen Christ in the forty days before his ascension to the Father. Hence, the constant return to the theme of the Transfiguration, for, even before the Passion, only three of his closest disciples were to see him once raised in glory on Mount Tabor.[1]

I have felt that the diktat of the Trullan Council required some outline for the development it set in motion. The prevailing histories of art inevitably underestimate its importance, preferring to see historical and stylistic development at the centre of their histories. It is a prejudice of naturalism that historians inherit from their culture. The theocratic society of Byzantium kept the place of personality in a state of innocent latency. It was precisely this innocence running alongside the elaborated and now sophisticated wisdom of the Church that accounts for the success of Byzantine civilisation in arresting history and giving stability to a theocracy. El Greco was the inheritor of this secure orthodoxy. Admittedly, deep cracks had appeared by El Greco's lifetime, and the days were long past when iconographers were required to be monks. Nevertheless, I believe El Greco's contiguity to those long centuries accounts for the ultimate simplicity and strength of his work.

The art of the Byzantines was concerned with contemplation, and the manifestation of the sacred through appropriate means. Their pictorial space is a direct inversion of corporal space to enable that unity of contemplator with his subject to bypass the distractions of sense and self. If the art of the Italian renaissance was concerned with the 'why and how' of sensation, the iconographer's art was an exercise of the imagination in its own world— the world as mystery and the archetypes that are its key. The Renaissance—in its best men—is concerned with the realisation of imagination in sensation. Byzantine art involves a renunciation and circumscribes by innocence all that would draw the personality into the relativity of sensation. The Renaissance as a culture could not last, for it was built on a knife edge between its Christian background and the possibilities for the self opened up by the exploration of sensation. About the most urgent choices in life very little is ever uttered. Nobody actually said that renunciation was too difficult, but from the point of view of the new science the possibilities for selfhood were too intoxicating. With his 'forgetfulness' a new fate for man had opened up.

The 'softening' activated within the melting pot of Crete was a slow and very unselfconscious process. At first it could almost be said that Western influence was a spur to the Byzantines on the island. To an artist like Angelos working in the 1450s it supplied a stiffening of Latin *gravitas*, but by the time of El Greco's birth evidence of the constructive absorption of Italian ways was not so convincing. In the end the old style could not absorb the new science. It seems that societies decay from the inside. What had been a respectable conviction or a worthy identity at one stage suddenly seems false at another, not because of a shortcoming in the intrinsic values of the old order so much as that some vital link in the chain of perceptions weakens. I mentioned that Byzantine art depended on a series of 'correspondences', in this case correspondences between God's power and our weakness. Baudelaire believed that such correspondences were the very foundation of poetic language. If poetic language is, as many of us believe, the very type of symbolic communication, then perhaps we may say that the strength in the chain that keeps symbolic language alive is a matter of delicately balanced inner life. It is not a matter of faith alone (much less will) but of inner perceptions and sensitivities in which the intellect and will are able to combine in unwitting sympathy. It is some such mysterious chemistry that allows certain great things to be done at times while leaving other long ages bereft of certain creative possibilities.

What sort of a man was Domenikos Theotokopolous? From a contemporary engraving he looks out at us from a neat but well developed physique with a bright appraising gaze. Perhaps the strongest impression from this engraving is one of aliveness. There is no trace of romantic soul-searching. We know nothing of his relations with his parents, or such details of his amatory life as would have been carefully cherished had he been born in the nineteenth century. All that has come down to us are a few stories. He is supposed to have infuriated the artists of Rome by saying that he could repaint Michelangelo's *Last Judgment*, and do it more 'decently'. Not from one story alone comes a picture of a certain arrogance: he was surely not the man to suffer fools gladly. In his heyday he is known to have enjoyed company and music at his table. Many record his wit, and that he was a boon companion. But he could also be frugal and solitary, and Pacheco, who visited him in his last years, notes his learning and his taste for philosophy. When he died, it is recorded that there was very little furniture in the house—only books and paintings. There were apparently many gentlemen's outfits, but no change of underwear. At his burial his contemporaries were sufficiently enamoured of his memory to write sonnets, epitaphs and verses. They may have been eulogistic, but never, surely, lugubrious.

History has pretty successfully obliterated the traces of his life story. We have mentioned how he worked as an iconographer in Candia until he was about twenty-five. There are occasional stories from his Italian years, but despite his apparent ambition those years show considerable uncertainty in direction until he arrives in Spain. In 1578 a son, Jorge Manuel, was born to him by Jerónima de Cuevas. His relation to her is one of the riddles of his life, as no evidence of their marriage has yet been found. A small painting records their life together rather fancifully; that is all. Jerónima seems to have died quite shortly afterwards, and from then on the child was brought up in his father's household. This would likely

22

have consisted of one or two servants, a studio assistant or two, depending on how good business was, and his faithful secretary and confidant, Francisco Prebost. The success and size of his studio varied, and stringency of means was no stranger to him. He had, however good friends in Toledo who helped him over a number of crises. Despite the difficulties of his uncompromising later style, the last fourteen years of his life were occupied with his largest and most remunerative schemes.

It is not unreasonable, from his art alone, to assume that El Greco was gifted with an original and sharp intelligence. He must have realised that the Byzantine culture of Crete was a spent force. Being a Catholic, it probably struck at his pride to see that the Italianate work being done on the island was not as good as the Greek: he must have sought a better way of being 'Western', or 'Catholic', than Crete could offer him. By his mid-twenties El Greco was an able practitioner, and once his mind was made up he had no difficulty in getting a recommendation from Maestro Damascinos to contacts in Venice. If we only heed the evidence of his ambition that would have been the course to take—to get out and make good the deficiencies of his own background. Rather than find himself in his old age at the head of a provincial folk style (for that was the fate that awaited both Greek and Western iconographers on the island), he chose to leap in at the deep end and master the evident charms of the new style.

III

THE GENTLEMAN ARTIST ABROAD

It is not certain that El Greco ever worked in the aged Titian's studio. To be accepted as a disciple it was sufficient at that time to be known to acknowledge someone as master. However, he studied the work of the three great contemporary masters in Venice (Veronese and Tintoretto completed the trinity) and produced a somewhat eclectic body of work. After some three years he went down to Rome possibly with the hope of good contacts in the ecclesiastical administration. There, surprisingly, he was registered in the guild of miniature painters, possibly through the influence of his friend Giulio Clovio, a Croatian miniaturist he had met in Venice. He studied the work of two *manneristi*, Beccafumi in Siena and Parmigianino (whom he continued to include in his pantheon of the great), and he admired the work of Bassano. While producing works which explore the Mannerist conception of dramatic and kaleidoscopic space he also accomplished that *tour de force* of realism, *The Boy Lighting the Candle* (fig. 1). The young Greco determined to try everything, but it was probably not until he underwent some spiritual or emotional crisis before leaving for Spain that he discovered the creative determinant that coalesced his scattered interests and carried him through the rest of his career.

El Greco always followed the Byzantine procedure of 'writing' his forms rather than building them. We see this in his early icons, as well as in the Modena Triptych where the entire surface is covered with coloured calligraphy to relate the inner and outer contours. In Italy he expanded within his own Greek idiom the range of formal information that the Italian 'builders' were insistent on including. In his six years in Italy he added to the skills of generic description, the suggestion of corporal weight and volume, perspective and, above all, the composition of space. Sometimes the writing is quite suave as in the *Christ Healing the Blind Man*

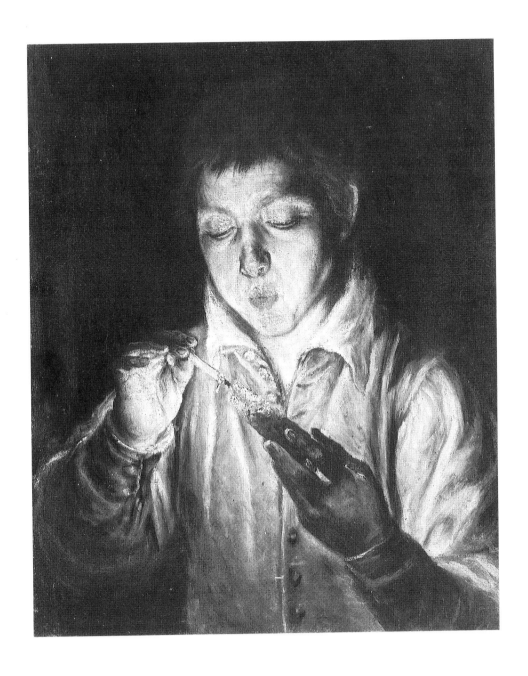

1 El Greco, *Boy Lighting a Candle*
Galleria Nazionale di Cappodimonti, Naples, 59 x 51cm

(fig. 8), so that one may overlook the calligraphy behind the surface, while at other times, as in his first *Purification of the Temple*, the calligraphy is of evident emotional force.

Italian artists must have found the Greek's art interestingly foreign. What they could not overlook, however, was the amount of Italian science the foreigner had absorbed. As an ambitious young foreigner El Greco was always jealous for his new-won status as an artist. Fine art was an Italian concept that was heatedly defended by theorist and practitioner alike, and El Greco appropriated this concept deliberately as a mark of culture. The financial rewards offered for his achievement at this stage would not have been great but they could be adequate for the modest requirements of a gentleman. Since a gentleman was one who, by definition, partook of a Classical education it was essential for Domenikos Theotoko-polous that he be not seen to slip back into that world of artisan craftsmen so much a part of medieval society east and west.

El Greco admired Titian enormously, but Titian was first and foremost a 'builder'. He composed carefully and intellectually by a long process of coordinating space and simplifying his composition. A contemporary description tells us how he would hide his paintings with their face to the wall for months if need be. Then he would put them back on the easel and '. . . look at them as if they were his worst enemy.' If surgery was called for, Titian would apply it ruthlessly. Surgery is, *pace* the medical profession, the remedy of the builder and architect whose concept is never complete until it is demonstrated in matter.

Of much more immediate import to El Greco was the example of Tintoretto. Tintoretto was a dyer's son who had made good by cut-price competition with his fellow artists. He was a man of boundless energy and drive, and had installed his testament over his door, 'The colour of Titian and the drawing of Michelangelo.' To resolve this dichotomy of allegiance he had developed his own brand of calligraphy and method of compressing a dramatic act in space. In fact, while separated by birth, El Greco and Tintoretto yet possess an uncanny resemblance as men. They were both cap-able, energetic and astute in the world, while at the same time being believers very concerned with the spiritual meaning of their religion and its relevance to the human situation in all its historical particularity. The method they adopted of relating the heaven-ordained contraries was one of quasi-poetic contemplation in which the events of salvation history are treated as total worlds. For both, the spiritual is not confined or typified by the ecclesiastical but manifests itself in the desire of the heart, a desire which holds the Christian in an anxious longing and a constant religious wonder. We know that El Greco studied Tintoretto's work, and we may be sure that study was not confined to the outward felicities of his style, but engaged in the complexity of Tintoretto's quandary.

Tintoretto is the master of the unexpected. Whether it is the milk that pours from the breasts of Venus, the privacy of Susanna that is rudely disturbed, or the confirming of the finding of the body of St Mark by the saint himself, the story is told in an image that is quintessential and compressed. The story seems to have been circumvented and the ordinary is discovered to be extraordinary. I do not believe El Greco ever forgot the legacy of Tintoretto. His painting of the *Adoration of the Holy Name* (fig. 2) is pure posthumous Tintoretto. The eye is sucked into a vortex of space, baffled, raised on high, and ends up mystified on the totally incongruous black figure of Philip II kneeling on a cushion in the foreground. The journey of the eye is accelerated through a maze of contradictions, and it is precisely through these bafflements that the exhalted emotion is held. It is an amazing access to the inner world such as might be vaunted by some surrealist of the 'twenties, but its determinants are not the plight of the individual but the relation of heaven and earth. Hesitantly El Greco rejected Tintoretto's space, but the anticipation of suspended emotion he learned from his example stayed with him the rest of his life.

Apart from the contact with Italian painters the biggest opportunity that Italy offered him in his six years there was the friendship with Fulvio Orsini. Orsini was librarian at the palace of Cardinal Farnese, a celebrated Classicist, and a correspondent with likeminded scholars all over Europe. Orsini was an intellectually curious and enterprising collector of painting and sculpture whose treasures numbered works by Michelangelo and Raphael. He possessed seven paintings by El Greco, no small mark of confidence in the Greek since their acquaintance lasted only three years. One of the preoccupations of Classicists at this time was the reconstruction of lost antique masterpieces from literary and historical descriptions. Some hold that El Greco's *Boy Lighting a Candle*,

2 El Greco, *Adoration of the Holy Name*
Patrimonia Nacional, Madrid, 140 x 110cm

probably done for Orsini, was just such a work of reconstruction of a painting by Antiphilus. As Jonathan Brown has written

> Cooperation between artists and scholars was not unusual in sixteenth century Italy. In fact the desire of artists to be considered men of learning and high culture brought them into ever closer contact with scholars like Orsini. The benefits of such collaboration were manifold. The men of letters put their knowledge at the disposal of the artists, assisting them in the formulation of learned subject matter for their paintings.[1]

Since so much of the classical world was available to the artist through writing, the artist learned to take for granted a special relationship between himself and the scholar. It may well be that El Greco's acceptance in the Orsini circle encouraged him to think of his art in more intellectual terms than would have been possible if he had already been engaged on fulfilling a string of demanding commissions. At the Farnese Palace he found himself in a charmed circle, and the respite that gave him allowed him the space in his life to piece together the extraordinary imaginative synthesis of form and colour that exploded upon the world five years later in Spain. El Greco was past his thirtieth year in Rome: he was mature enough to use the bonus fate had offered him.

When he was about thirty-four El Greco set sail for Spain in the hope of employment at the Escorial. He had contracted no major commission in his six years in Italy, and it must have seemed to him that he faced middle age with little to show for those years.

Toledo gave El Greco a worthy home, but brilliant as Toledo was intellectually, artistically you could almost say it was 'frontier' territory. At least in Crete there had been the last flickerings of a sustained visual culture. In Castile, however, the studio system was parochial, traditions had been broken by the wars with the Moors and only in the Northern kingdom of Catalonia did the studio system of the Middle Ages rise to any heights. In one way this was fortunate for El Greco: he had no rivals. In another sense, however, he bore alone the onus of introducing to the Toledans the modern and unaccustomed concept of art as a mediator of knowledge. This accounts for the recurring and time-consuming litigations that dogged the length of his career in Toledo. He claimed the financial rewards of an artist in the 'modern' sense of the term as he understood it. His clients, who were not so dumb as to miss the advantages of the modern thing they were getting, agreed to the price, but when the work was finished they reneged on the agreement because this master's prices were not what they were used to paying at the provincial studios. El Greco was obdurate because his identity as a 'modern' was at stake along with the authority of the values he had assumed with his Italian training. Compromises there had to be, but Domenikos Theotokopolous remained the gentleman artist who was 'learned', and a bit of a philosopher, till the end of his days.

1 El Greco, *The Assumption*
Art Institute of Chicago, 401 x 229cm

2 El Greco, *The Arrest of Christ*
The Cathedral, Toledo, 285 x 173cm

3 El Greco, *Ss. John, Evangelist and Baptist*
Museo del Santa Cruz, Toledo, 110 x 87cm

4 El Greco, *The Crucifixion*
Museo del Prado, Madrid, 312 x 169cm

5 El Greco, *The Resurrection*
Museo del Prado, Madrid, 275 x 127cm

6 El Greco, *Laocoön*
National Gallery, Washington, 142 x 193cm

7 *Pentecost*, Novgorod School

8 El Greco, *Pentecost*
Museo del Prado, Madrid, 275 x 127cm

IV

THE PAINTINGS

Toledo 'gave El Greco fame', and he in his painting gave it such unforgettable form that it is difficult not to see the city through his images. As the River Tagus makes its way across the plateau of central Spain a great rock causes it a convulsion that forces it into a circular detour before it springs back on its westward course. Toledo rose on this rock. Wherever you are in the city you are conscious of the floor of the river's defile and of your height above it. All around the city are small parks and squares where you see across the gorge to the restless heights beyond. The impression is of a landscape that has lost its middle distance; it has been sucked down into the gorge where the river flows unnoticed. There might be a slight promontory in the foreground and then the distant rise and fall continues immediately from it. It is this landscape that gave the artist the space and background for his figures. The saints portrayed rise to their monumental proportions while the distant perspective shoots back from their feet. A horizon line is never defined but the tumbling movement of the distant plateau continues into the enlarged clouds and sky. So insistent is the artist on maintaining this rhythmic continuity between the landscape and its inhabitants that all along the contour, at judicious points, he will have the sky rubbing shoulders with the saint portrayed. Other parts of the sky will be allowed to recede, but somewhere else along the contour the artist will inevitably drag a bit of his cloudscape forward. Aldous Huxley described the experience of entering El Greco's space as like being inside a whale: you have just enough room, round where the sky meets the rocks, to scratch your ankle. Elsewhere the sky is like a skin pressing towards you. The eye is forced to stay on the surface—to stay with the being portrayed.

All great art depends on some analogy of sublime simplicity between life and the craft available, an analogy simple enough to reverberate through all the possibilities of personal life. Such an analogy was the one El Greco discovered on his arrival at Toledo. The landscape where the middle ground had been spirited away became a natural home for the saints, a landscape between infinity and a perpetual 'now' of the foreground plane. Here he could find a background to his saints as appropriate as the gold had been in Greek icons, without archaicising his newly acquired science.

1. *The Assumption*, Chicago Art Institute

The Assumption (pl. 1) is the centrepiece from the first great sanctuary ensemble that El Greco made on his arrival in Spain. It was commissioned by the dean of Toledo Cathedral for the embellishment of a new funerary chapel in the prestigious convent of Santo Domingo el Antiguo.

The whole ensemble of seven paintings in the main altarpiece and two small altarpieces to the left and right of the sanctuary area was to be a paean of praise to the sanctity of the body of Christ. The celebration of our Lady's assumption into heaven was to remind the faithful that she had been the first tabernacle of the Lord's bodily presence in the world. The ensemble was to be crowned by *The Holy Trinity* (fig. 3), now in the Prado, manifestly demonstrating the Father's acceptance of the Son's sacrifice in a corporal representation of the dead Son resting on his Father's knees. These themes were all to add up to a major statement of Tridentine theology. There are many erudite nuances to be found in the relations of the different parts of the retable that bear witness to the unity of purpose between the client and the artist, while we may be sure the dean had his own reasons for exemplifying this theology in Toledo where elements within the Church were still restrictive in their attitudes. However, if El Greco was conscious of a role as propagandist he never lets us know. His treatment of this elaborate symbolism is never literary or academic. The symbols work subterraneously under the amplitude and confidence of the forms. We do not read them intellectually, but experience them through the life of the form, unselfconsciously.

If Christ in his earthly sojourn possessed a body akin to ours, then that body could not have been a stranger to its own weight.

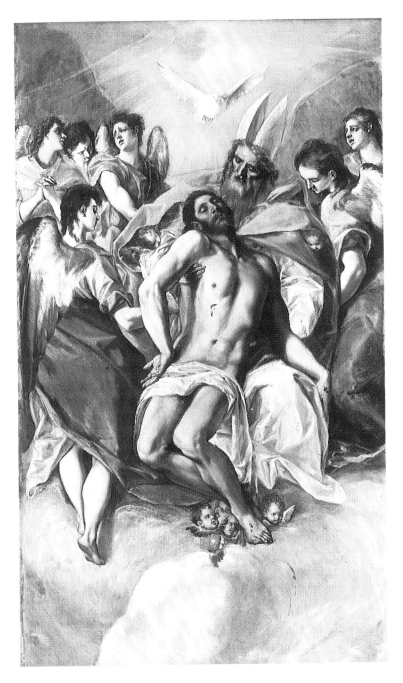

3 El Greco, *The Holy Trinity*
Museo del Prado, Madrid, 300 x 178cm

Hence the Council was not averse to the new degree of skill in the artistic representation of bodily weight. The great achievement in this altarpiece was for the painter to have demonstrated these new skills to 'make real' without any loss in the spiritual temperature of the scene portrayed. Science has given these figures natural weight and body, while imagination has lifted this tangible weight so that it floats heavenward. The feat of the new science has been accustomed to the grace of imagination, and imagination has learnt a new exaltation at being able to accommodate so much within its own truth.

The Assumption follows the dual schema of many other paintings of El Greco's new found maturity where the heavenly and the earthly regions are sharply separated half way up the canvas. Only the hem of our Lady's garment, draped over the moon, links the two self-sufficient areas. Our Lady dominates a tightly knit group of angels (treated rather like a low relief sculpture) which swirls and spins towards the heights of heaven. The apostles left on earth are divided into two equally close knit groups by the classically moulded sepulchre from which our Lady has risen, the only architectural feature in the painting and one of cool absoluteness. In the bottom right hand corner St James the Greater grasps the book that is symbol of his theological status in the early Church. The rest of the apostles form an arc around this sepulchre, their heads representing the most extraordinary animation of space. They seem to stand on the edge of the world, witnesses to an event where history has been made redundant. The sight has set up among the apostles the most eloquent ripple of wonder ever described in painting. This is the wonder from which theology will be born.

The structure of the volume and space in *The Assumption* could be described as 'musical' rather than representational. Two great cylindrical volumes act as the main themes—our Lady above and, below, an apostle with his back to the spectator in to the left foreground (possibly St James the Less). To continue the musical analogy, all the other figures are like subsidiary themes, or the development sections of a sonata form to these two figures or motifs. The concept of the painting is everywhere built up elaborately on a series of long low-slung arcs. The forms described by these arcs spring from each other. The angel to the right of our Lady seems to spring from under her armpit. The hem of that angel's garment describes a similar arc, and the same arc is to be found under the angel who kneels on the far left. It is amusing to keep a tally of the number of times this form has been repeated. The use of these arcs, however, is never just a linear construction. Quite the opposite: the formal conception of the painting is of great balloon-like floating masses. What the arcs do is assure the continuity of the form, the empirium of airborne existence. The lines that describe arcs are everywhere broken so that the contour has the impression of linking the forms rather than identifying and separating them. The depth in the painting is not as shallow as in his later work, but it is quite as systematically curtailed through the device of abutting edges between sky and figure. It is as though the figures and their background were knit together in a vast concave/convex movement of the surface. And even if this concavity is imagined with the aid of a contour line at the point of the picture's greatest depth (behind the moon) it would describe the same arc as all the others.

The drama of an infinite perspective was one of the essential tools of expression of the Mannerist painters working at the time of El Greco, so why did the artist of *The Assumption* limit his use of distance so drastically when his own interest was so palpably dramatic? The evidence, I believe, testifies that El Greco saw himself portraying a sacred drama. That is why the brush-work in the heavenly region is so full, and the brushwork in the earthly region is so nervous and broken. The two clusters of the apostles' heads accompany the deepest points in the penetration of space. Yet it is precisely at one of these points of depth that the artist jolts the space forward with the cheek of the man who abuts to the hair of the main foreground figure, the apostle with his back to the spectator. All the drama of an infinite perspective has been expressed, but without the use of perspective. El Greco's is a kaleidoscopic space which is both infinite and on the surface of the canvas at the same time. His figures are at once burgeoning into being and contracting into the infinite. That is what eliminates the sense of space as we describe it in nature and assures us of the figure's other-worldly source of vitality.

El Greco's attitude to the sacred drama is strictly classical: the human figure in space is the only vehicle of expression. The only things that could be described as 'props' are a moon, a book and a tomb; and yet the sense of a scene evoked is more powerful than anything in Carravaggio. The similitude of the figures would not have such power over us were it not for the totality of the space the artist conceived. The mystery described is grounded in the light of the intellect. Even as beneficiaries of the new Italian science we can be sure that the exalted subject matter of the Church's tradition will not delude us.

2. *The Arrest of Christ (El Espolio)*, Toledo Cathedral

In the *Espolio* (pl. 2), as it is popularly known, a luminous and voluminous red Christ is surrounded by a motley crowd of soldiers, disciples and riff-raff, menacing but ignorant. In the foreground to the left hand side, on a steeply sloping piece of ground, are the three Marys. On the right hand side opposite them is a functionary who bores a hole in the wood of the Cross. It is a mêlée of some twenty-two souls from all walks of life. In this mêlée Christ is inviolate and incorruptible.

The painting was immediately recognised as a masterpiece, although it promptly plunged the artist into a legal dispute with his clients over the appropriateness of the iconography. The canons of the cathedral claimed that since there was no evidence from scripture that the three Marys had been present at Jesus' arrest, the painter had taken an unwarranted liberty by including them in the picture. The dispute was prolonged and eventually the artist said he would paint out the Marys. This was never done, however, to which happy weariness of disputants we can be grateful to this day.

Whereas in *The Assumption* El Greco dealt with a mystical theme whose only source, aside from the experience of the Church, was the Book of Revelation, in the *Espolio* he had to treat with an historical act. Other imaginations would have quite legitimately given colour by showing the bridge over which the soldiers crossed, or dwelt on the human impatience of St Peter. Instead of that, El Greco singles out the moment of maximum spiritual experience where Christ forgives his persecutors—'for they know not what they do.' El Greco's originality is in the directness of his treatment, but his apprehension of the dramatic act is as classical as Greek tragedy.

There is no concession allowed by the artist in involving the spectator in this central moment. We may identify with the three

39

Marys as with the Church present, but their presence is only a leitmotif and a foil. The simple arc made by the back of the man who prepares the Cross hurls us into the mystery of Christ's red robe. The foreshortening of this figure to the right compresses the space, but also compresses the time: hence the urgency of our encounter with the main character of the drama. When we have got over the shock of this first encounter, and the mocking violence of the green-clad thug who binds our Lord, our eye wanders into that extraordinary crowd of soldiers and apostles, loafers and common criminals, that undesirable sea against which Christ's pale head floats like a beacon. It is one of the most celebrated passages of 'realism' in the whole history of Western painting, yet it is necessary to recognise the artifice behind this corporality and the spiritual purpose that directs it. When we stand back from this sea of spontaneous and bravura brushwork we are struck by the symmetrical disposition of the axes on which the heads lie. They constitute an array of jabs in alternative directions. One or two heads at the sides are shown in profile, but the rest are shown three-quarter face. Only the figure a little to the right at the back, who, pointing, alerts the soldiers to the man to be arrested, shows a full face. The heads immediately above Christ are all larger in scale than his head, a device the artist uses with his usual purpose of keeping the vitality of his 'actors' from seeping into the distance, but the front-face figure that points is again a 'jolt' of space that is doubly poignant for its unexpectedness. It acts as the catalyst for the paintings 'low-relief', and as a pivot for the diagonal movement of all the other figures. The compositional structure of the *Espolio* is not as 'musical' as *The Assumption*, which no doubt has to do with the historical nature of its subject matter, but the control of the volumes on the surface is equally rigorous and the interplay of the contours just as subtle.

If the *Espolio* has possessed the imagination of countless generations of spectators it is because of its perennial contemporaneousness. The sixteenth-century furnishings, such as they are, present no historical barrier; strangely, what possibly strikes the most historical note for us is the face of our Lord whose upturned eyes recall certain tastes in Counter-Reformation piety. Yet this head of Christ is sensitively mobile, and the gesture that accompanies his blessing assures it of sublime authority. The painting is haunting in the distinction it carries of the contingent from the abiding, the ordinary from the extraordinary. The artist who conceived the crowd behind Christ knew the 'ordinariness' and triviality of human malice. He knew its banality and its good intentions, its innocence that is at once culpable and pathetic. In this awful and potentially wonderful 'ordinariness' Christ is the 'single one'. What is inviolate is ever alone. The act of God's forgiveness is never understood by men: it is always separate and pure, because it is the spirit's own action. Man's destructiveness in the china shop of his world is powerless to destroy. It is as though our real spiritual innocence is a measure of our failure to exist, to really, in some sense, 'be'. If there ever was an attitude we call 'Catholic Humanism' then this picture must be its most potent expression, because here we see the possibility of the humanity Christ offers us, and the desert where we are without.

The *Espolio* was completed in 1579 and El Greco fulfilled only two other large commissions in the next ten years: *The Martyrdom of St Maurice and the Theban Legion*, and *The Burial of Count Orgaz* for the Church of San Tomé. There is no lessening of power in these, but the intellectual and geometric approach to form is more relaxed. It is during these years that he commences that series of paintings of Ss. Francis and Dominic—and other single figures—that continues in production till the end of his career. Devotion to the saints was a feature of Counter Reformation piety and it is likely the artist saw a new outlet for the work of his studio in fulfilling a need. Some are studio works for which he probably produced a cartoon or an underpainting. In others he would have painted the head and final details. In a lot of cases, however, these *santos* are authenticated as having been painted by the master, and we recognise them for the nervous spontaneity of their pathos. As relatively uncomplicated compositions they gave El Greco the chance to experiment with his brushwork and with the very personal language of forms for which his later work is so celebrated. The development of this language, however, was emphatically reserved for paintings of sacred themes and personages. Throughout the course of his life his religious work was accompanied by portraits for private clients. Unfortunately the scope of this book cannot include them, but I commend them to the reader. They are remarkable for their realism, their sympathy and their wit. Their understatement strikes a curiously modern note in the spectator, as does the terseness with which the painter establishes the nervous mobility around the mouth so that it partakes in the eyes' gaze. Velazquez, who, since he could not see the need for sacred themes to be cast in a special vessel of form, did not appreciate the master's religious works, admired his portraits as second to none.

Before going on to discuss some of the later works it would be as well to look at the master's procedure with colour and understand some of the problems he had with it. Historically colour has been the poor relation of painting for so long that the case of El Greco, an artist universally accepted as 'a colourist', often receiving contumely because of it, can be revealing. Colour is a complete language and will not sit down with drawing unless drawing has had the modesty to relinquish some of its more utilitarian functions. El Greco was one of the first European masters to recognise this. He believed that the use of colour was a vital issue for the painter. However, although well aware of Michelangelo's limitations as a 'colourist', he did not himself quite manage to overcome some of the more entrenched habits of the men who followed after Michelangelo. By saying this I do not wish to challenge his repute as a colourist; with certain historical hindsights, however, the reality of his difficulties with colour have to be acknowledged.

In his early work, and in certain individual works throughout his career, El Greco was prepared to allow colour its full force in the middle tones. This is the region where colour has its greatest saturation and density, and its greatest expressive possibility. Thus, when he allowed the red its full saturation at the heart of the *Espolio*, the symbolic analogy of its use, coupled with the emotional content of the painting, is unforgettably forceful. In all these works his use of colour is symbolic, not in any sense that can be read intellectually, but in a purely emotional way. The glowing reds, the sulphurous yellows, the sour greens unite to establish a sacral world, a world beyond graphic description, a world that only refers to our world analogically.

'Graphic description' we say, as if drawing told us how it was. But, of course, for the painter of an imagined theme there can be no graphic description—only more or less telling analogies by which a range of experience can be shared. The painter has to begin somewhere and so he begins with yesterday's analogies. How he adapts these is everything.

El Greco began with the human figure fired with a serpentine or flame-like grace (inherited from the Mannerists) and clothed in a loose Gothic drapery. In his early Toledo work he adapts this inherited analogy with a brilliant completeness and rigour to his own sacral purposes. As he gradually insists more and more on the disembodiment of his figures, however, the Gothic drapery becomes like a writing with light. The great *Espolio* in Toledo Cathedral possesses its full resonance of colour, but in later versions the colour has been curiously bleached out. The centre of the form (known in academies as the 'third edge', the point of the form closest to the spectator) is like a lightning conductor. The third edge is so bright as to have no colour, while the real colour only exists marginally between the highlight and the colourless shadow into which everything else is plunged.

It is known that El Greco was concerned that the figures in his paintings should be seen as 'heavenly luminosities'. Without doubt he was versed in the thought of the Pseudo Dionysius, with whose *Celestial Hierarchies* he was familiar. Here it is only necessary to note the general principle of its metaphysic—that the lesser luminosities of heaven transmit the light of God from him to us. El Greco was not concerned with the luminosity of objects lit from a direction, but with objects who bore their luminosity within. If for the painter colour is the agent of light, for El Greco the treatment of colour was critical. It was, then, to some degree anomalous that El Greco continued to use the idiom of modelling with light and shade that had been developed by the Mannerists of the late Renaissance. It was this anomaly that drove the painter in his later work to break up the mass of his forms into a rippling field of small lights. If he had become aware, as Matisse and Bonnard three centuries later became, of the power of colour modulation itself to create form, his art would have developed in some quite other way. As it was, El Greco, so far as he could, made a virtue of historical necessity.

The later work involves us in the enigma of El Greco's solitude, and the profound intransigence of his pursuit of his art. For the present I will be content to make two more or less practical reflections on the artist's situation within his times. El Greco was a celebrity. He was the single figure who mediated the modern art of the Italians to the Toledans. He was acquainted with all the influential minds of the Counter Reformation in contemporary

43

Toledo, and their identity was bound up with their acceptance of his work. With the astonishing works of the late '70s and '80s he made many loyal friends who, if they were unable to follow him to the full extremities of his thought, felt it only right that his thought should be given full rein. But to many those extremities were not unfamiliar; they were, for instance, the currency of poets like Góngora, or spiritual writers like Alonzo de Orozco, with whose writing we know El Greco to have been acquainted. Perhaps the ultimate success of a painter (to himself) depends on his adaptability to solitude. El Greco's art is a flight of the highest and most disciplined imagination, but this 'flight' is totally vain if the painter tries to make it serve himself. At this level the painter must leave himself open to serve a purifying process that imagination has begun within him. 'The inner life on which the painter has meditated during his long hours of solitude penetrates the substance of the painting, and itself becomes the painting', as Lionello Puppi eloquently puts it. In his later work the eclecticism of his Venetian period, his appreciation of Tintoretto's surreal sense of the unexpected within the ordinary, his memory of Byzantium and its theocratic purpose are all made to subserve an attenuated and deep meditation. Cassou, writing in 1931, has compared El Greco's late style to the 'conceited' verse of Góngora, where artifice is used to reinforce a state of mind. 'The bombast and solemnity of these verses, the rarity of the expressions, the drawing out of the syntax, alternating with sudden abbreviated forms and the suppression of articles, which give greater weight and intensity to the substantives, his way of blocking his sentence in such a manner as not to let the mind relax or take breath. . . ' correspond at every point to the way El Greco constructs his late masterpieces.

3. *The Two Ss. John*, Santa Cruz Museum, Toledo

On a hillside near Toledo stand the two Ss. John—the Evangelist on the left, richly clad in crimson and blue, and on the right the Baptist, with a mere animal skin supported from his right shoulder (pl. 3). John, the friend of Jesus, draws the attention of the Forerunner to the gold chalice in his hand from which rises a phoenix, symbol of rebirth to eternal life. The Baptist listens and points to the rough bamboo cross at his side. The two seem joined in a conversation without words—not so much a conversation, perhaps, as a revelation to each other of mutual and complementary being. Each is attended at his feet by the appropriate symbol, the Evangelist by a mysterious eagle and the Baptist by a Lamb who nestles at the foot of the cross.

The flickering light illuminates a low relief and the drawing joins the figures in a continuum. However, as always there are surprises. Here the buffeting forward of the form occurs where two folds describe the calf of the Evangelist's leg next to the eagle. The dark of the eagle is the most mysterious tone and almost has the quality of being a 'black hole'; beside this the Evangelist's leg separates itself in a radical forward movement. It is this jolt that draws our attention to the two complementary and characteristic spaces inhabited by the two saints—the one quiet and pastoral, the other dynamic and explosive. If the whole of this painting is like the musical and abstract development of two characters, the humble Baptist and the apocalyptic Evangelist, where would we expect to find the key to this characterisation but in the attributes assigned to each saint. The cross of the Baptist is painted with extraordinary poignancy. It has no weight, much less power in the world, and the crossbar is only attached to the stem with a casual piece of rough twine. It is simply the most elementary thing a desert father might have made for himself. Contrasted to this is the richest symbol of divine and sacrificing love for man, the wrought cup. The Baptist's is the craven and hollow-eyed love of the human soul raised against its will by the divine *eros*, whereas the Evangelist's is a hallowed sharing in which time and space are shattered by the divine gratuity. The sky behind the Evangelist bursts through the frame indicating the alliance of the apostle with the Good News that bursts through time from eternity.

The extraordinary achievement of El Greco is to give us all this as 'being' and vision rather than as something to be read by the intelligence. The living and varied flame of the form works on us like a musical analogy for the inner characters inhabiting the painter's world. The meditated rhythm of the painting is working on us long before we are intellectually ready to question it.

As suggested earlier, from any strict theoretical point of view we are forced to admit that El Greco never quite reconciled his treatment of colour with his vision. He did, however, side-step the problem in many paintings by the sheer force of his conviction, and by his poetic sense. One solution was to treat the shadows themselves as surface. The shadows are not cast by any particular direction of light but are part of the overall flickering luminosity which convinces by the nobility of the artist's drawing. So long as the shadows in the painting are not too extensive (as in, say, a large painting like the late *Assumption* in the same museum), the eye accepts them as light in movement and the figures and their world co-exist on equal terms. The solution is knife-edged: at any moment the shadows may reveal their origins in the Tenebrosi, and weigh the painting down with the vacancy of corporeality, or the high-lights may remind us of nothing more than the grease paint at the theatre. These traps awaited the artist on his off-days, but we may respect the difficulty of the tasks he set himself.

4. *The Crucifixion*, Prado Museum

The Crucifixion (pl. 4) now in the Prado was probably[1] painted in the early years of the seventeenth century for the Seminary of the Incarnation in Madrid. The seminary was set up in the 1580s at the bequest of Doña María de Aragón by Fray Hernando de Rojas and Blessed Alonso de Orozco as a model college for the Augustinian community. *The Crucifixion* is thought to have been part of a retable of some three to six paintings (depending on whether they were meant to be displayed in a two-tier or single-storey format) set up to commemorate Blessed Alonso as founder of the college. Alonso was a man of formidable sanctity who commanded the widespread respect of society from the poor to the king himself, in whose confidence he was held. Since he was also a widely read author of mystical writings and tracts in sixteenth-century Spain, it may be considered inevitable that the artist's clients would in this case have acquainted him with the writings of the friar whose memory he was to celebrate. So what is the relation of El Greco's work in *The Crucifixion* to the mysticism of this now forgotten friar?

The Crucifixion has always struck me as a unique work in the artist's output. It is a painting of some ten feet high and unusually monumental for his later style. The presence of three of the most eloquent angels in Christian art distinguishes it from any other crucifixion he painted, and helps to establish a sublime calm that eludes the exaltation of his other work. To what extent is this uniqueness due to Blessed Alonso?

Alonso's thought was based on the assertion of the afore-mentioned Dionysius that it was only by figurative analogies and veiled similitudes that the human mind could be illuminated, an attitude whose Classical genesis and authority we have forgotten. The difficulty of Alonso's writing for people of our time is the literalness with which he developed his figurative analogies from Scripture, applying them to the state of mind of saint or prophet or faithful. When we hear of the altar in church being 'the crib of the Christ child' our minds balk at anything so strong, and all the options so precious to our freedom tremble in the wind. It is yet possible that such analogies are only the proper grist of such a Catholic imagination. For instance, Alonso's interest in the Annunciation to the Blessed Virgin was as much in the anguish of our Lady's inner life, as in the message being transmitted to her. 'According to Alonso', writes Richard Mann,[6] 'the Virgin enjoyed free will like all other mortals, and could have rejected the divine commission to become the mother of Jesus. Alonso imagined that Gabriel's announcement had provoked a "great battle" within Mary's spirit. . . . The Virgin's active role in the Incarnation was demonstrated, Alonso claimed, because the Father engendered the Son in her womb only after she uttered the miraculous words: "Behold the handmaid of the Lord; be it unto me according to Thy word".'[2] All Alonso's efforts are directed to making the figurative analogy 'carry' the spirit of Scripture with the maximum corporeal force. To have Mary's freedom described to us like that, to have put the reality of her obedience to God in such realistic terms, is both sobering, and not a little humbling.

From time immemorial, and in many traditions besides Catholicism, angels have been seen as the mediators between God and man. Possibly it is only in a proud intellectual Deism that angels are not deemed necessary, since only they in a heavenly constitution can rend the veil between him and us while sparing our destruction. For Alonso they were totally real: he talked with them, he adored the Host with them and, as we have seen, his theology was concerned to exemplify the wonder felt by Gabriel at the 'fiat' of Mary before God's word. He believed that angels had been present with Christ all through his Passion and that they had even, as he picturesquely put it, tried to gain some 'accidental glory' from it by washing their hands in his blood. Since Alonso held that angels were unable to create the Son miraculously, or to consume the elements of the Eucharist, it follows naturally that for the angels attending the Crucifixion to receive the blood of Christ in the liturgical cup would be inappropriate.

In this painting by El Greco, Alonso's theology of angels is adhered to quite graphically. The group of Mary Magdalen and the angel at the foot of the cross is likewise a direct transcription from Alonso's writing. Such a humble service to God as cleaning his cross could, Alonso asserted, make Christians the spiritual equals of the angels who also adore him.

The first impression made by *The Crucifixion* is of a living symmetry. The disposition of the figures defers to custom with such formality that the eye could easily be lulled from noticing the very unconventional things that are going on. The scheme of the form is hierarchical with Christ as the main theme, Jesus' Mother and St John as a dual secondary theme, and the Magdalen and the three angels taking up the subsidiary themes. The stem of the cross travels the full height of the painting so that, though it is hardly described at any point, it maintains a potent presence. The sky is dark with a slight cloud formation in low relief emphasising a diagonal configuration. Behind the Blessed Virgin is a massive bank of cloud whose blurred edge runs parallel to the edge of the cross. There are, unaccustomedly, no meandering cloud shapes, no random holes of blue sky.

The form of the Prado *Crucifixion* is extraordinarily grandiose, but quite without taint of the human transcendence that usually clings to that word. The sense is of a sublime purpose expressed with poignant economy of gesture. In the prevailing continuity of its form it is close to *The Assumption* from San Domingo el Antiguo. The gestures, set in wide sweeping forms that encompass and embed them, raise the eyes slowly heavenward, from which perspective we contemplate the pale body of Christ. The zig-zagging of the plane closest the spectator (which we have found such a feature of the painter's late work) has here been subdued, and the forms have been allowed their full volume. As in *The Assumption* of twenty-five years earlier there is no naturalistic distraction to soften the tension between gravity and grace: it is this tension that makes the airborne sensation of the forms so compelling. Only in the angel to the right of our Lord's feet is there a moment's nervous flash of highlight dance. All is solemn consummation of a sacred destiny in the meeting of the horizontal and vertical arms of the cross.

Dominating all, the haunting and pale body of Christ hovers triumphantly. Richard Mann has much to say about El Greco's realism[3] in treating the suffering of our Lord. He claims this to be in response to Alonso's theology of the suffering Christ, a theology which we can surely now acknowledge to be tainted by a too human sado-masochism that, incidentally, had a disastrous effect on the later development of religious imagery. It is true that the painter crossed Christ's right foot over his left, a historical detail that would, Alonso held, have caused the weight of the body to fall directly and painfully on the wound. I suggest that El Greco complied with Alonso's 'fact' but persisted in painting the body of Christ according to his own spiritual vision. El Greco's view of the pain and violence meted out to the High Priest and all who follow him was one of classical restraint: we dwell not on the suffering of the martyr but on the faith which inspires his witness, and not on the faith alone, but on the luminous point that inspires that faith. The body of Christ in *The Crucifixion* anticipates the resurrected Christ. It anticipated its pale inviolability, and its separateness from all other bodies. El Greco could not paint this 'inviolability' by describing a body but only by the telling analogy of making it spin in its own life. El Greco brings realism only to the small specifics—such as the historical notice attached at the top of the cross. All that pertains to the sacred is expressed in pictorial and symbolic 'correspondences' made living by their pervasive musical rhythm. At the top of the painting the artist compares the rectangle of Pilate's notice to a vivid parallelogram of cloud on the left. There they sit like two portents isolated from the rest of the painting by the bar of the cross. Perhaps it is this cloud shape that assures the Christ figure of its autonomy. It is like the hand that with one flick of wrist unleashes the energy of the lasso, or like the device on a spinning top that sets off a perpetual motion. It initiates a spinning movement down the body of Christ to the hand of Mary Magdalen emerging from behind the cross. The dynamism of the body of Christ is assured of recurrence in perpetuity because of the device to which it is attached. As El Greco must have known from his Greek background, the more spontaneous a surprising analogy is, the greater is its force.

It does seem that El Greco's response to Alonso's writing was double-edged. Where Alonso's metaphors and analogies make real the distance between God and man in the unction of the gesture that crosses that distance, El Greco finds support for a vision that is mystical; but where a human naturalism in any way abuses the devine unction of that distance, El Greco quietly leaves Alonso's sentiment to one side and pursues the course of his own vision. There is no doubt in my mind, however, that El Greco made a special sort of effort when he came to paint *The Crucifixion,* and that Alonso's writing acted as a catalyst. The work is redolent of the most fine tact. It reserves its power to hold our attention from the awareness and psychic energy that made such tact possible. The angels in this *Crucifixion* who receive the blood and water from Christ's side into their hands move us because they respond to the divine economy. If one drop of that blood is sufficient to save the whole world, it must require the infinite solicitude of angels to save what is so precious. El Greco's painting is about that high solicitude.

Modern man feels distinctly uneasy with the word 'unction'. It reminds him of something a great-aunt might have given him at Christmas. This frightening word only means 'anointing'. Whoever and whatever the agency of it, the blessing comes from above. The wonderful gift of that generation in Spain, the generation of St John of the Cross, St Teresa of Avila, and of El Greco, was to have somehow glimpsed the structure of a divine unction. Somehow they sensed the steps in the infinite distance of God from man in such a way that a sacred language might scale those steps. How special the divine unction is we may glean from the rather less than divine unction we find in later painters, like Murillo. There the unction is our own. We would like to feel good about holy things; we know that we fail to, but we cannot separate what we really feel from what we would like to feel. The divine unction, on the other hand, is God's own. God cannot be divided against himself, and so his unction does not cloy. Quite the contrary, God's unction comes to us as the most pure playfulness. That is how El Greco communicates to us the gratuitousness and freedom of God.

5. *The Resurrection*, Prado Museum

A pale Christ bearing a white banner rises from a hollow in the foreground where a soldier has tumbled, overpowered. In a narrow space there are some nine figures being flung back in disarray by the blinding light that has accompanied Christ's rising. Most of them are soldiers, rough men wearing some rudimentary clothing, but one man in blue, on the right, seems to have a different function. He is surely the member of the faithful with whom we are meant to identify.

If *The Crucifixion* is an elaborate icon of the central event of Christianity, *The Resurrection* (pl. 5) is like an instant snap-shot from a well placed camera within the tomb. The matter-of-factness of Christ's body almost makes us feel that we are intruders. *The Resurrection* was painted during the same period as *The Crucifixion* and I am tempted by the supposition of Professor Perez Sanchez that it was intended as part of the same 24' high (six piece) retable at the College of the Incarnation in Madrid. There are hardly two more disparate works in El Greco's career, but we may well ask if the disparity is not complementary because of their subject matter. *The Crucifixion* is like an inward meditation: its whole tone is gathered and recollected. *The Resurrection*, on the other hand, is extrovert, almost peremptory, as though conceived as a ten-foot lightning sketch. The two works have the ability to make their subject stand outside history, but in quite different ways. A historian of art might trace history in the analysis of *The Crucifixion*'s style, but I believe El Greco's intention is to baffle such an enterprise. So inward is the meditation here that everything that might give a temporal clue is gathered towards its eternal purpose: the 'historical' is shorn from it. It is as though the matter of 'times' were gathered together to the one point were their meaning is made secure. *The Resurrection*, on the other hand, takes place in an eternal 'now': it is time reversed, contradicted from within time. It is as though in the first painting the artist were a monk who has secured the crucifixion of his God at the heart of time, while in the second he is a journalist who records what happens always, every day, in every man's life.

The sense of 'event' makes *The Resurrection* one of the most exciting of El Greco's paintings. The arrangement of the tumbling soldiers' legs acts like the petals of a flower of which Christ is the stamen. The comparison of the strange flaky light behind Christ (one of the most extraordinary depictions of exploding light in the history of art) with the same light reflected on the foreground soldier makes a perfect foil for the pale Christ. The blue on the right introduces us to the general golden luminosity, while in the centre the cool greys of the far soldiers separate the area reigned over by risen flesh from the area of our fallenness.

We must, however, face the possibility that, imaginatively, the painting is not entirely resolved. The problem ultimately concerns the 'matter-of-factness' of something so exceptional as Christ's risen flesh. Who put in the shadow under Christ's right armpit, a tone so noticeably cooler than the shadows that model the rest of the form? How unlike the master to include so incidental a shadow! Was it that only in the shock of an extreme realism he could express the transcendent upturning of the soldier's world? Or was it an insistence that flesh, when taken up in the risen God-head, is flesh indeed? As an image, *The Resurrection* is unforgettable; as a meditation, it is, perhaps, ambiguous. It is like a question thrown at us, that of our very nature we are unable to answer. Christ's flesh is supreme and inviolable, but we may question whether its incorruptibility is totally convincing.

If the supposition of a two-tier retable can ever be finally demonstrated, we must wonder at the enormity of the labour of the now aged painter, and at the overpowering effect that so comprehensive an expression of Tridentine theology must have had on the spectator.[4] *The Crucifixion* would have dominated the top story, and the bottom story would have had as its centre-piece *The Annunciation*.[5] Ever since Counter-Reformation times 'The Annunciation' has been called in Spanish '*The Incarnation*'. The whole retable would have been seen as a celebration of God's custody of our human nature. The doctrine of the body as the temple of the Holy Spirit, the sacramentalising work of mortal flesh undertaken by *The Incarnation*, was perhaps the central pre-occupation of Counter-Reformation theology. We feel it lurking behind many of El Greco's paintings from the elegant and immacu-late body of the dead Son who lies over his Father's knees in the Prado *Trinity* to the works we have now been discussing. We see the artist treat Christ's flesh as the meeting place of the Father's condescension and our humanity. Perhaps it is this doctrine that above all forced El Greco to desert the sure steps of medieval iconography that dominated the imagery of his youthful background. There is an existentialism, a personalism, implied in the doctrine of the divine flesh difficult to resign with the systematic cosmology of scholasticism. Unlike the world El Greco would have received with his youth, where the analogies between heaven and earth were fixed, the world he gives us in his later work is like a fluid two-way-stretch between a barely glimpsed heaven and deserted humanity. In this fluid world Christ's flesh is like the mustard seed mentioned in the parables; it is the 'one small thing' that betokens the possibility of our true humanity. Those who like to call El Greco a great 'humanist' are correct in one way: he is the celebrant of the great possibility that Christ confers on human flesh. On the other hand they would be gravely mistaken to suppose that this 'possibility' is any less hidden within us than the mustard seed is within the earth, except to the eyes of faith.

6. *Laocoön*, National Gallery, Washington

Since Laocoön was an unfrocked priest of a faith other than Christian I will have to ask the reader's indulgence for letting him in a side door at the end of this chapter. *Laocoön* (pl. 6) is the only theme from classical mythology that El Greco is known to have painted. He painted it for himself, and originally three versions were found when the stock of his work was listed at his death. No academic has been rash enough to hazard a reason for the painter's departure from his customary thematic material, but I believe that common sense suggests that for the artist it was a sort of swan song or epitaph.

Laocoön had been a priest of the Trojans. He married and had two sons and it was for this he was deprived of his office. A few days after the Greeks had lifted the siege of Troy, Laocoön together with his sons and some citizens went out onto the plain in front of the city to offer sacrifice to Poseidon. It was Laocoön who first saw the great wooden horse standing by the foreshore where the ships had been. The citizens were all for bringing the horse into the city, but Laocoön warned them. 'Trust not the gifts left by the Greeks.' The citizens argued with him, no doubt reminding him of his priestly incapacities, whereupon two great serpents came out of the sea and attacked the disgraced priest and his sons and killed them. The other citizens immediately understood this to be a sign of the gods' displeasure with Laocoön and dragged the horse on its wheels into the city—to their celebrated undoing.

The foreground of the painting is filled with a great rock on which the aged Laocoön struggles with the serpent. To the left the arched and full-length figure of his son struggles with a second serpent, while to the right, at Laocoön's head, his other son has fallen dead. Three citizens at the right watch this curious unfolding of destiny. In the background is a splendid cityscape of Toledo. There was a tradition still alive in El Greco's time the Toledo had been founded by wandering Trojans, and it is quite possible in the unfolding of the drama that Troy is a metaphor for Toledo. The horse is drawing up to the Old Bisagra Gate, which is still the main entrance to the city on the Madrid side. Above is one of El Greco's most portentous skies which repeats the splayed gesture of the main figure and absorbs the diagonal of the dead son's body into itself. The work is virtually monochromatic and three small areas of blue sky are the only alternative to an overall tonality of brown and grey.

The atmosphere of *Laocoön* is of a perennial enigma. Everything is closely knit together—rocks with men, men with land, and the land with the sky. It is in that sense analogical with a tragic destiny where things do 'conspire' against the truth of the individual. All the inhabitants of the painting are naked, as befits the primal condition in which God set them down on earth. If the scene we witness is a tragedy, it is notable for the lack of rhetoric in the poses of the figures. These men have not 'measured all things'. It looks more as if they have been tossed on the rocks and left there. There is a peremptoriness in their poses which is only saved from indignity by the obvious involvement of the sky with what happens on earth: what takes place here has been allowed by the Gods. Laocoön is suppliant (his head is very similar to an earlier *St Peter Repentant*) but unavailing, but his son on the left is defiant even to the point of death. This is a quite extraordinary figure for its sense of recurrent movement. El Greco, as we have seen, never dwells on pain or violence, yet here the point of contact between the serpent and the victim is one of intense dramatic presence. The complementary arches of the man's body and the serpent's seem locked together. The contrast of the serpent's efficacy with the tragic inefficacy of the son's defiance are put down with the abrupt authority of one for whom life and death are reconciled, a man who sees them both in each other.

The peculiar treatment of the dark area that delineates the son's arm was a gesture of immense significance to countless moderns. In fact the arm vanishes into its own darkness as irrevocably as the futile gesture it describes. The boldness and power of such a visual analogy is something that would not be attempted by artists again for over three hundred years. But the fact that El Greco was able to treat form in so abstract a way when all around were so careful to substantiate their visual analogies with naturalism, shows the immense confidence he had in his own vision, his firmly intellectual grasp of what the visual language would take.

What does *Laocoön* mean? We shall never know, and I do not believe it matters either to the artist or to us. The valuable thing to us is the experience of time's mysterious coexistence. El Greco, for whom doctrine and thought mean so much, never gives us his thought in discursive form, but as vision and experience, couched in thought's emotional equivalents. The painting, like the story, is about the perennial conditions that exist between men and the gods. Christianity does not automatically make such a speculation redundant, as witness the trouble that has striven in the very bosom of the Church down the ages. The scene of the unfaithful priest turning out to be the true augur, and of the gods who destroy him in his very moment of truth, is a double irony that may possibly have had some meaning for the artist within the incomprehensions of his contemporaries. I am sure El Greco was not the first old man to speculate why we men make over the prophet's words to our meanings, and destroy ourselves with the signs of God.

V

MANNERIST TIMES AND THE PLATONIC INHIBITIONS

El Greco regarded painting as an enterprise in the pursuit of knowledge. This was the revelation of his Italian sojourn. Even though local artists in the Toledo which hosted El Greco plied their craft without such pretensions, there were many educated citizens who were prepared to take his work on his own evaluation, and who were able to share in the perspectives opened up by it. But the 'knowledge' that El Greco credited to painting was not just that pertaining to the natural laws acquired during the Renaissance. It also comprised the theological knowledge of the reform movement we now call the 'Counter-Reformation'. Extraordinary to relate, El Greco was the only artist to take the concerns of this movement convincingly to heart.

Modern art criticism is a development of nineteenth century criticism which was almost totally absorbed with the categories of naturalism and their relation to the artist's sensibility. When El Greco's works were rediscovered in the last century there was no intellectual background to which they could be related. Their power was felt, but because of the distance of modern Europe from the specifically Christian and Catholic concepts of the sixteenth century, critics tended to concentrate on the extraordinary 'matter' of the paintings to the neglect of any intellectual content they might have. The selectiveness of their critical approach was, of course, governed by the nineteenth-century view of the intellectual plausibility of religion as a whole—which was that it had none. In the nineteenth century the concepts of science were allowed to take religious concepts to court and try them according to their own law. By this crude process the knowledge and wisdom of Christianity were disallowed any intellectual content and were shorn of all authority outside the subjective one of our own hearts.

By this ruling, 'intuition' was personalised and the arts were driven to the subjectivism and aestheticism which have typified them for our time.

Catholicism provides a subtle and wide-ranging intellectual structure for the faithful to cope with their experience. In studying the work of El Greco it would be vain to let any contemporary prejudice discount the value of his structure in coming to an understanding of his work. El Greco's concept of knowledge may be only 'intuitive', but it will be meaningless unless we accept it as part of the whole structure of Catholic teaching in which it is bedded. Mysteries of religion such as the Virgin Birth, Man and God united in Christ, or the activity of sacraments, cannot be understood by anything less than the 'speculation' (as El Greco called it) of intuition. 'Intuition' for the Catholic is not inhibited by doctrine, because it partakes of the same content, the same 'knowledge'. The 'faithfulness' or orthodoxy of an intuition does not rob the knowledge gained of its authentic truth, or, for that matter, make less 'intuitive' what is known. It is, I believe, only the all-pervasiveness of certain assumptions of modern criticism that has heightened for us the solitude of El Greco's position within the European heritage and appeared to deprive him of the community he shared with the intuition of his time. The nineteenth century within us may not approve of El Greco's concept of 'knowledge', but for El Greco to posit an intuitive art was a normal thing to do in his age.

It had been done before by Michelangelo, whose influence in the sixteenth century was unavoidable. It is well to remember here the problems caused for artists and patrons alike by that series of discoveries in the skill of painting to attain verisimilitude during the period from Masaccio (d.1428) to Michelangelo (1549). How far were these discoveries appropriate in depicting the life of Christ and the saints? The more one individualises the participants in a universal drama the harder it is to maintain its universality. How can one sustain the emotional temperature fitting for a sacred representation while flattering one's patron with a vivid profile of him coming up the steps? Painters were not insensitive to the problems they encountered: they heatedly recommended their own solutions, and positions were taken. The position that Michelangelo adopted was that painting and sculpture partook of the universality of poetry and myth. By the mental act we describe as 'intuition' the artist conceives a world which takes its symbols from nature, but is otherwise an artifice of his own. The validity of that world lies in the unity of its emotional and imaginative temperature, and the consistency of its space. Michelangelo, like El Greco, had very definite ideas about art, which, we are told, peppered his conversation, but in a busy life they were never committed to writing. We know he was widely read in 'poetics' and a strong component of his thinking was probably his ambition to equate the two arts and bring to the visual the status of the word. We know his attitude in that ever-recurring dispute between the 'measure' wrought by the artist's eye, and those who advocated the use of rules and calipers before the model. He believed in the authority of the artist's eye. To take a measure to get a head 'right' was to betray the authority by which the rest of the figure had got its vitality. El Greco quoted Michelangelo on the authority of 'the artist's eye' and was obviously indebted to him in the liberties he himself learnt to take. But above all was his debt to Michelangelo's supreme example in making a universal art based on poetic intuition, and for restoring the idea of art as invention in the days when those who espoused the cause of art as the 'mirror of nature' were heady with new triumphs.

Alas, Michelangelo was only partially successful in his aim to make a mythic art. First of all he was not a painter but a sculptor. This meant that his greatest imaginative effort was made under protest in an art form he abjured. More importantly, he satisfied only one of the criteria for those who are so rash as to intuit an imaginative world. He satisfied the unity required by the emotional temperature of his figures to live a convincing life, but he placed them in a vacancy, a 'no space' where they rattle about without a home in heaven or earth. So powerful was Michelangelo's personality, so humble his sincerity, that the next generation swallowed his art whole. Not being poets like the great man, they tied themselves in a terrible knot—and Mannerism was born.

El Greco, for all his indebtedness to Michelangelo, never lost an opportunity to disparage the master's paintings. His admiration for the atmosphere-soaked painting of Titian forbade him to make those allowances for the great man that his Roman contemporaries made. El Greco had been tutored in 'painterly painting', a craft of brushwork in which the world has to be a totality, and the totality has to be made sensible. In Venice he had learnt what colour can achieve and the utilitarian role that Michelangelo assigned to colour in his frescoes must have seemed a wilful demeaning of its function. When the academies finally stamped Raphael's indifference to colour on European painting practise, colour was shoved under a mat of fateful orthodoxy. Every time a colourist was born the constant simmering between the colourists and the draughtsmen would flare into a battle royal. Now that the academies have been routed, however, and the dust of many misunderstandings has settled with the victory of the colourists, perhaps we may allow El Greco's percipience in calling a coloured drawing by its true name without disrespect to the master who made such an extraordinary thing of it.

The example of Michelangelo greatly complicated the practice of those who came after him. They missed the fundamental simplicity of the great man's spirit and turned his artistic bequest into a series of technical and aesthetic problems to which they applied themselves myopically. It was a period of *cadenza* art when the painter showed off what he knew—his expertise in foreshortening, his acquaintance with the antique, or his ability to make startling compositions with groups of figures. It was a time of intense intellectual polemic when artists and savants began to speculate about the artistic process itself. Granted that area of liberty in the 'liberal arts', greatness does not usually accommodate itself to succession. The achievement of their predecessors was a drain on the spirit, so painters took refuge in the 'interesting' and the novel, which is a certain hell that can await them betimes. El Greco shared in these sophistications and anxieties, and it may well be that, were it not for his Cretan background, he would have survived them no better than his contemporaries. The greatness of his predecessors was not quite his problem in the same way it was Rosso Fiorentino's or Beccafumi's; to be Greek could be an incalculable advantage. But he was a son of his time and he believed, as they did, that the 'glory' of art lay in tackling the most 'difficult' artistic problems. The apparently effortless solution of such a difficulty denoted the possession of *grazia*, a hard word to translate but suggesting the beauty of the spirit made visible demonstrated by an apparent facility. It is noticeable that El Greco's praise of *grazia* contains no alarm comparable to the apprehension the word 'facility' now raises in artistic breasts. For us 'facility' brings with it the suspicion that the object and content of such ease of execution must be derivative. For El Greco, however, the solution to difficulties with *grazia* was a mark of the intellectuality of the artist.

Throughout his career El Greco is at pains to find the irreconcilables and to reconcile them. The possessor of one of the most controlled techniques ever mastered, he is always anxious that the brushwork appear fresh and spontaneous. He sensed that the appearance of spontaneity was what most helped the spectator to share the form depicted as an experience, in distinction to the appropriation that a hard-edged verisimilitude might inspire. This scruple was a constant for the duration of his artistic practice. An example of this control within apparent freedom is the early *St Veronica* in the Santa Cruz Museum at Toledo. The face is painted with a nervous sensibility suggesting the tenderest solicitude, while the veil that lightly frames it is painted like gossamer with a rapid flickering notation. El Greco was able to do a second version (in the Caturla collection) without any sign of labour or loss of the acute sensibility of the original work. It is evident from this that El Greco did not look on spontaneity the way our culture does. Spontaneity in his eyes did not exist for the self-expression of the artist, but for the spectator to share more immediately and sensibly in the content of the subject matter. It was for El Greco an attribute of the artifice of the world the painter created in his picture, an extra dimension to its 'seeming'. Once again his thinking was in line with the ideals of the age, this spontaneity being just an aspect of that 'facility in solving difficult problems' in a way that gives delight to the spectator. It is worth remarking, however, that the brilliance of El Greco's brushwork is quite different in intention from a naturalist's like Velazquez. Velazquez' brushwork will serve to bind a homogeneous world in one atmosphere, while in a painting by our master all the parts will be consciously painted in a variety of ways to characterize their dramatic role and meaning in the work as a whole.

Another major preoccupation that El Greco shared with his time was his delight in the *figura serpentina*, which the critic, Lommezo, claimed to have discovered it in the figures of Michelangelo. He noticed that a certain flame-like spiral movement animated the figures created by the great man. This was seen to bestow on the figure its *furia* or soul, and was conceived by the Mannerists to be a sign of great vitality. Its prestige was immense and it is to be found as a basic unit of almost any Mannerist composition of the sixteenth century. El Greco's use of it is unique because in his work it becomes a regenerative symbol in its own right. It contains the symbolic analogy felt unconsciously by all those who have attributed a mystical intention to the artist's work. Alert as one becomes to El Greco's own intense self awareness and deliberation, I see no reason quite to discount this association simply because it has a genesis in the aesthetics of the Mannerist period.

If the foregoing seems to show how much El Greco was a man of his time, it would be quite misleading to see him circumscribed by it. The *cadenza* art of the Mannerists found a very uneasy place in the Church, whereas, by a happy alchemy, when El Greco tossed all these contemporary preoccupations together he made them subserve a form and content that were deeply Catholic. Before we discuss his art in relation to its religious background, there is a further matter in which our own period is indebted to his canny percipience: I refer to the 'difficulty of colour'. It was not just that El Greco sought out the formal and technical difficulties of his chosen art form. Beyond that he sought out the very difficulties of the visual language for the painter itself.

There is no doubt that the primitive and original act of man-the-artist is to draw. Drawing comes from pointing. When man has identified an object of his interest he points at it, and if the chap beside him is a bit dumb he naturally grunts some exclamation and describes what he is looking at by following a contour with his index finger. This Adam makes his first drawing. It is as though there had been silence and now there is a word, but better than a word, because it has a 'likeness' to what is described. This is not the 'magic of verisimilitude' but the magic of recognition which precedes it. For original man it is magic indeed, for he is then able to identify the things he needs and plot their acquisition. This is good for 'active' man; it is not so good for his brother, contemplative man, for how is he to restore what he has identified to the great cosmos from which he has just torn it? Drawing separates, but colour unites what has been separated. Colour erodes the edges of drawing and marks the relationship of things. Colour remakes a cosmos of relationships by a sensible and formal analogy between those relationships and its own.

El Greco saw that dichotomy plainly in the two main traditions of painting in Italy, the Florentine and the Venetian. He realised that although hundreds of Florentine painters used colour, and many used it with some taste, the true role assigned to it was merely to reinforce the drawing. Down in Rome they followed the Florentine practice, with the added sophistications that we have described. Alone among his Roman contemporaries El Greco held that the virtuosity required for drawing spectacular foreshortenings still falls far short of the intellectual unity to be established through colour in treating space as a totality. Hence the artist's insistence at the edges of his figures, that the colour binds the figure to its background. Likewise, when El Greco uses the strongest contrasts of tone the effect of the opposition is of unity rather than disjunction. Ingloriously the academies of art that sprang up in the sixteenth century perpetuated the errors of their Florentine and Roman fathers teaching colour as an adjunct of drawing. El Greco's insight remained unexplored till the advent of the Post-Impressionists and the Fauves at the commencement of our own era.

There is a further significance in El Greco's election of colour above drawing. This has to do with the prevalent Platonic reservations about the acquisitiveness encouraged by the artist's verisimilitude. If drawing has the special role of identifying things in the world, then drawing has the special responsibility for forestalling the acquisitive impulse in the spectator's reaction to the image before him. The way that most artists of the High Renaissance overcame this moral reservation was by Idealism: the things identified by drawing would be so 'noble', so purified of their accidental charms by their reinvention as generalised and universal 'forms' that nobody's acquisitiveness would be unduly stimulated. How original then was El Greco's solution to, what some might deem, a Platonic inhibition! By insisting on the unifying role of colour—that colour creates worlds, not identities—he was able to bypass the whole ponderous idealism of High Renaissance representation, and posit a visionary world which would be an equivalent of the Church's teaching.

II

If art panders to our weakness through its illusions, how will we find an art of abnegation which will not confirm man in his weakness?

That, of course, is Plato's question, and it has haunted Christianity possibly more than it haunted Antiquity. If Christianity is not content to rest with the Judaic prohibition of images, it of all religions must have the clearest mandate for their use. In practice, from the demise of the monkish art of the iconographers, the mandate of the Church to the artists was very tentative. The painters contemporary with Dante presented no problem to the Church for the ingrained habits of a medieval liturgical symbolism—in studio and out—kept the sacred nature of the artist's task before him. By the time of which we have been speaking, however, science had made the artist first, bold; then, with the prestige of class and fame, positively wilful. The Church was taken off its guard and, beyond insisting that the figures in the paintings be properly clad, it did not know what to do. It lacked a principle in which the new science could be subsumed to its theology. Both El Greco and Raphael owe their fame to the peculiar responses they gave to this need of the Church. As we have seen, by the grace of genius El Greco found the ingredients which made his solution so convincing at home in the contemporary age. Adhering to the taste of the age they helped him to 'bed' the new theological concepts in an acceptable way.

In view of the importance of 'similitude' for the Western tradition of painting it is as well to have some idea of the proclivities and inhibitions of the Antiquity from which it was born. Of all the cultures present in Antiquity the Greeks were the people who best mastered the techniques of verisimilitude. Their attitude to it, however, was far from one of simple relish.

Similitude in painting has a bewitching quality for which the best of us are unprepared. The cherries that look as if a bird would pluck them out of the picture, the Dutch still-life bread whose crispy edge makes you want to eat it, are the uncomplicated pleasures whose innate response defies our examination. We simply do not see what is happening to us. Similitude is like a magic where the world is given back to us vicariously. It was precisely in the unwonted vicariousness of our response that Plato sensed a danger.

If the arts are about a vicarious life where we may meet ourselves in a mirror, the scope for painting's delight is not limited to cherries or Dutch bread, but extends to the complex depths of our desires. Plato saw that this magic could be a close agent of idolatry. He wanted us to desire only the Good, but since the Good is unrepresentable, the mimetic urge itself should be scorned by any true seriousness. For Plato, obedience to that law of gravity within us that plummets us towards pleasure was the greatest weakness.

We could possibly accuse Plato of puritanism for never allowing that the artist's likeness of the world could be a recreation of the world in Love, a transformation in which the world is divinized through the continuation of God's creation. Plato only credits the culpability of our acquisitiveness, he only sees the danger of our vicarious pleasure, never the divine potential that lurks therein. While in no way allowing Plato the last word, I believe we have to take seriously the searchingness of his anxiety. That noble fastidiousness within him was unwilling that man should be short-changed with counterfeit dreams. His anxiety reveals the deep moral and metaphysical ambiguity that confronts the painter in similitude. The painter, he suggests, who would correct this ambiguity, the vicariousness of resemblance, must develop an eye of the soul, an 'inner eye'. With Plato, superficiality is the peculiar sin of the artist, and the territory where this particular daemon is confronted is 'similitude'.

Modern man looks on existence as a horizontal affair in which all aspects from the delightful to the worshipful compete for our attention on an equal footing. That was not the attitude of the Renaissance, nor of the Antiquity to which they deferred. If we wish to understand them we must suspend that relativism by which any priority allowed is deemed exclusive. Earth was seen to reflect heaven as its inverse—created to Creator. In this scheme Man is the erect creature who reflects in his standing position the Father's image down on creation. It is man and the angels who conduct the intercourse between the antipodes. This intercourse is, of course, infinitely multilayered, a fact that does not affect God or matter, but affects man's pilgrim way. Plato's anxiety was that we should misread the layers, that we should attribute to the heavy breathing of our sighs a more glowing content than they possessed. To forget our mortality was to insult God's eternity; but likewise not to admit that which exceeds us, or not to wish to exceed oneself, that was spiritlessness. Sadly that is also our wretched programme of relativism, and the Christian/Platonic order (to whose duration we can ascribe some one thousand seven hundred and fifty years) regarded it as the very 'definition of Lucifer'.[1] Indeed, Toledo saw itself as a fortress for the Good as also for the Person of Christ who incarnated the 'Good' in a way whose intimacy Plato could not have guessed. The emotional life of Toledans was involved in a spiritual warfare whose heroic symbolism reached into every sphere of their daily lives. It was assumed as automatically as the premise of a cultural identity. And while, no doubt, some measure of chronic Forgetfulness lingers in all such automatic assumptions, we should be careful to root out some of our own before we judge them.

I believe the beneficence of Plato's anxieties to the West should be admitted. His thought acted as a cement for medieval theologians, affording them a flexible psychology that kept the issue of the moral life alive. It gave the Church an intelligible floor space in the middle ground, between social and personal life, where the Church could meet the world, and it acted as a brace against the subjectivism that would sweep Europe after the French Revolution. Finally it gave us (tempered) the work of El Greco, and with Raphael (1482–1520) the exemplar of a Catholic European style that lasted, somewhat battered, till World War One.

To realize the hold of Raphael over European taste you only need to read that entry in Delacroix's diary where he very tentatively entertains the judgment that one day Rembrandt may be found to be Raphael's equal. Raphael's peculiar synthesis has lost its hold on us because we are no longer concerned with the dichotomy it was to reconcile. The appetites of our taste have been so pluralized and relativized by the 'reproduction boom' that we have forgotten the passion with which, for past generations, taste was beholden to 'truth'. For us the relation of taste to truth is more complex, but, if it is outlawed from the judgment of intellectual acts, it is still the infallible indicator of the ability of the will to absorb them. The scruple of taste works underground to establish the new act of will to itself.

It all goes back to the thorough job that Raphael did on Pope Julius II. In a most charming way he sold him a brand of Christian Platonism. It was a very tempting concoction politically—modern, classical, elevated and polite. Nature was to be studied to enable the stage to be set for a new, responsible and converted humanity to act on. Phenomena were to be sifted through Greek eyes, and a synthesis between naturalism and idealism offered that at last the

Church could call its own. The Church was suffering enough from the waywardness of artists making their discoveries at its cost, but here was a methodology that would allow the Church to order what it needed and to receive what it expected.

The trouble with this wonderful synthesis is that it was a designer's ideal, the willed art of a great draughtsman, who selects from history a sterilized and universal humanity. Look at the Borghese *Deposition*: it is a tinted drawing engineered for balance to the last diagonal. The reds and blues of the draperies are mechanical enough, but what really disinfects the oleographic air of this painting is the colouring the flesh. The weight and density of hue throughout the limbs and heads of the group are unvaried. There is not one accident of sensation that could make the scene alive for us.

Perhaps a more serious criticism of Raphael, as an artist of the Christian ideal, comes with hindsight from the discoveries of our own contemporaries. They have learned that 'written' forms can be just as moving as observed forms. Rather than create an elaborate reconstruction of phenomena to express an imagined state of event, the direct and naive putting down of symbols may be a more immediate analogy for the mind's eye (cf. fig. 4). Imagination does not need the drawn-out paraphernalia of phenomena to make its own hypothesis. For the 'tellingness' of vision, omission is more crucial than inclusion. From this point of view Raphael's peculiar thoroughness in 'picture building' strikes us as academic.[2] Much more spiritual for us are the dramatic narratives of the so-called 'Primitives', the icons of Eastern Europe, Macedonian wall-paintings, Carolingian miniatures or Romanesque sculptures—indeed, nearly all the art that was conceived innocently of Renaissance science and the Platonic will to be 'elevated'. I must admit that, typical of my generation, I cannot but blench at that much loved image, the *Sistine Madonna* of Raphael (fig. 5), an image in which we first surmise the wretched destiny of a humanly-willed world. An icy wind blows through that conscientious but unwitty work.

Fortunately I am not alone in this, and Andrey Tarkowsky's testimony[3] offers reasons clearer than mine. He points out how the Virgin Mary 'is an ordinary citizen, whose psychological state as reflected in the canvas has its foundation in real life: she is fearful of the fate of her Son, given for people in sacrifice. Even though it is in the name of their salvation, he himself is being

4 Karl Schmidt-Rottluff, *Christ and the Adulteress*

5 Raphael, *The Sistine Madonna*
Staatliche Kunstsammlungen, Dresden

surrendered in the (Madonna's) fight against the temptation to defend him from them.'

All this is vividly conveyed in the picture, but from Tarkowsky's point of view, 'too vividly. For the artist's thought is there for the reading all too unambiguous and well defined. One is irritated by the painter's sickly allegorical tendentiousness hanging over the form and overshadowing all the purely painterly qualitites of the picture. The artist has concentrated his will on clarity of thought, on the intellectual concept of the work, and paid the price: the painting is flabby and insipid.'

Significantly Tarkowsky then quotes from a letter of Gogol's: 'it is not my job to preach a sermon. *Art is anyhow a homily*. My job is to speak in *living images*, not in arguments. I must exhibit life fulface, not discuss life.'

It is possible that in quoting the late film director, Andrey Tarkowsky, I appear, having first extolled Plato, to contradict the value of any precept in art. Nevertheless, precepts make a dangerous guide for the artist, and what is specially dangerous is the literal application of them. In art the ideal—which is only the idea of the best, a bare concept—has to be translated into Gogol's 'living images'. How you do that is open to question: that it must be done is the rule of art. The difficulty with Raphael's work is that it satisfies Plato's strictures more in principle than in fact. It is true that where Raphael generalizes and amplifies his forms he holds them above the thraldom of an egotism that similitude could immerse them in. The forms have the amplitude of their application in an elevated Gospel narrative. Instinctively, though, we know that the Gospel situations did not feel elevated 'to themselves': this 'elevation' is something we human beings give them in the concept we have formed of them. In the paintings of Raphael this concept is peculiarly complete, but its very completeness secures it against the accidents of life that would bring it alive for imagination. The completeness of concept in Raphael is a piety, and as such it belongs, not to the sacred figures portrayed, but to us. In the end piety is a poor conductor for the divine to work through. The 'devotional' only reflects what is ours back to us. We need to gaze on that which draw us, the transcendent. We are not brought there by our own motor.

Raphael's art presupposes a converted Christian society without describing the wherewithal by which that humanity is converted.

Where the inhabitants of El Greco's world are ordinary temperaments on whom the Holy Spirit has wrought, with much extremity of experience, its own conversion, the inhabitants of Raphael's world are well educated idealists who have chosen their Christianity. Alas! their choice has protected them from the extremities the Holy Spirit might visit on them. The failure of Raphael may well have been to supply a cultural answer to a religious problem. That is possibly why today we find the religious content of his painting so unconvincing. Once the Renaissance synthesis he offered is seen in its historical context, the authority of the style that became associated with the Church suffers the contumely that descends on that invidious choice.

The piecemeal dismembership that Renaissance Idealism received at the hands of various streams of Western naturalism took generations before Raphael's persistent hold over the European consciousness was broken, but once the limitations of his solution to the needs of Pope Julius II were perceived, the solution that El Greco provided to essentially the same problem would reveal its peculiar conviction.

The eclipse of El Greco's own reputation almost immediately after his death was, I believe, due to the later developments of the Counter-Reformation. Round this time the latest style to be imported from Italy was the dark realism of the Tenebrosi, heralded by Caravaggio. Painters found a cinematic way of the high-lighting the dramatic act by plunging most of the canvas into darkness, and then drawing the act out of the darkness in a vivid and individualised realism. It was a shock tactic that appealed to evangelicallyminded clerics. It lent itself somewhat too easily to scenes of martyrdom and, since it is always easier to elicit an emotional reaction from men than ask of them a real act of contemplation, a numbers-conscious Church came to favour it above other styles.

A VISIONARY ART
WITHIN THE CHURCH

I

Often taken as an example of the mysticism typical of El Greco's art, *The Burial of Count Orgaz* (fig. 6) hanging in the little antechapel sealed off from the rest of San Tome, creates an impression from which hardly any visitor to Toledo is exempt. The painting is a celebration of the virtue and efficacy of charitable acts (upon which Calvin had cast some doubts) whence the redoubtable count is honoured at his entombment by the miraculous assistance of St Stephen and St Augustine. The painting is divided half way up by a row of heads, each cocooned in the ruff typical of the Toledan gentry of the day. Above this the panoply of Heaven opens to receive the soul of the count, while in the foreground his body is being respectfully lowered by the martyr and the doctor of the historical church into a sepulchre originally situated below the painting. Manuel Cossio, who wrote one of the earliest studies of the artist, described *The Burial of Count Orgaz* thus:

> The subject is not in itself mystical, but merely religious. . . but what is mystical is the interpretation, in the most real and direct sense of mysticism, because every element in the painting, notwithstanding the transparent realism, is treated ecstatically, mysteriously, and devoutly. And not only is there mysticism, but Castillian mysticism, because, starting with a funeral story of purely local interest. . . and ending with the murky hidden background, all is inward, intimate, serious, sad. All is inward-looking, all is essentially common-place, and the corpse, the saints, the monks, the priests and the gentlemen all appear as if enclosed in their 'inner dwelling' and rejoicing in it.

Cossio's eloquent language is well suited to express a poetical idea, but I wonder if it would be acceptable to anyone privileged with a mystical experience. The Spain of the time of this piece of writing was suffering a major crises of identity, and a retrenchment of the national spirit. Cossio himself was one of the 'Generation of '98', a group of writers and artists who felt indebted to El Greco as an example of the national spirit, passionate, mystical and austere. If there was a shortcoming in their appreciation of El Greco, it may have been in the certain poetic of the work that they grasped to the exclusion of the content and matter of which it was but part. I propose that we should take mysticism seriously. Many people have had mystical experiences and I see no reason to scorn their testimonies because one's own experience holds nothing comparable to theirs. But we must be precise too: all we can be sure of is that El Greco was a painter. There are no diaries, there are only works of art. The work of art places the experience it describes in a parenthesis. The theme of a painting is something described for our contemplation. It does not thereby become denatured, but the imagination has recreated whatever might have been the experience of the man behind it. I see no reason because of this to say that the 'as if' proposed by the work of art is purely aesthetic: only mathematics is that. But once the painter has transformed his triangles and cubes into living geometry, they are burdened with the real emotional possibilities through the equivalents and correspondences recognised by imagination. These 'equivalents' do not beat us over the head; they merely await our growing.

I suspect that if you were in receipt of mysteries you would find Cossio's interpretation unserious, maybe frivolous. To separate an act of charity from the mystery of God and attribute it to the rule of religion would at least be tendentious theology. But possibly the whole tone of Cossio's nationalism offends you. To propose a Castilian mysticism is immediately to suggest that the subject is a mystic because he is a Castilian. Mystical vision is a free gift addressed solely to the receiver, an onerous sweetness permeating his personal faith. What makes a Christian mystic is the mystery of the God/Man, Christ. The mystical experience is of the bride with her lover and its authenticity resides solely in the gratuity with which the ineffable distance between them has been bridged. To propose a natural mysticism is immediately to wipe out that gulf chasm—to say that those light years that the Lover has so

74

lightly traversed never existed. True love can only exist within the category of free choice. Tell a bride that her feelings are due to genes and chromosomes and you have shorn her of the only self-image that can support her. No doubt of its nature the world will always speculate about lovers. The speculation of art, however, always has a certain impersonality: whether we regard the experience in El Greco's paintings as personally his own, the question for the artist is not whether something 'happened', but in what way such a happening is constituted.

Nature, of course, is subject to divine transformations at times. If nature is the creation of a Creator it must be so. We feel very strongly that it is so, and that is where national mysticisms can be misleading: our own pantheistic urge to transcendence becomes so easily confused in them. The major body of El Greco's work, I believe, shares in a very pure spirituality, but it is possible that the universal appeal of *The Burial* owes a debt to something less pure. The poetic condition that Manuel Cossio describes so eloquently belongs not to the Church's spiritual repository, but to a magic moment of history when El Greco's friends vicariously attended the count's funeral, providing the painter with that row of discrete heads pitched in undertaker's black, at the centre of his painting. It is they who cast the prevailing atmosphere of a heroic generation over the obligatory and timeless obsequies of the Church. Nevertheless there is a certain unresolved ambiguity about the presence of these gentlemen. There is perhaps just a slight 'knowing' in the melancholy fervour of these citizens, a certain self-regardingness in their piety. There is no malice or satire in El Greco's representation—just a sparing economy in the telling of the way we were then. The ruffs, the artifice of a civilization, are symbolically effective in isolating the human beings behind them from the miraculously aided ceremony they witness. There is the suggestion that perhaps their 'inner dwelling' is not quite what they thought it was.

Of all El Greco's large paintings it is fair to say that *The Burial* is the least typical of the master. It is the only one in which he allowed the world of his patrons to obtrude—a habitual Renaissance flattery that he had resolutely turned his back on. It is the only painting he made for a public place of worship, all his other work being seen only within closed communities. Further, it was the only major painting theme to which he never returned as was his habit with all the other themes he treated. His constant harking back to compositions has nothing to do with a menial repetition required by his clients, but with the imaginative authority bestowed on certain compositions by their sacred theme. In this realm of creation in the borderline between two worlds, Sir Kenneth Clark observed that 'once the image is charged with its meaning it need not, or must not, be varied.' *The Burial* is an immense 'sport', an occasional piece of Shakespearian proportions in tribute to its times, but it does not quite carry the spiritual authority of some of his other works. The immaculate and tender recording of the two heavenly visitants, Ss. Stephen and Augustine, as a statement, does not quite survive the pyrotechnics of the upper regions.

It is fitting to commence a discussion of El Greco's relation to the teaching of the Church with a look at his most famous painting. It is the painting by which most people identify the artist, and if we have been able to sort our way through some of its ambiguities we may be on a better track for exploring the general nature of the work El Greco undertook.

By the end of his life El Greco must have been theologically very 'literate' because all his schemes for altarpieces bore instructive purposes that had been discussed in detail between the artist and the client. There is no evidence that El Greco balked at such close cooperation with his clients, and his signed contracts bear witness to the right of the patron to terminate the contract at the first sign of displeasure with the work accomplished—a legal position which, understandably, would not be tolerated by our contemporaries. El Greco must have had a great self-confidence which in its turn must have comprised a shared experience with his clients across which they could understand each other—a psychological position rare for our contemporaries. It was very important to the Tridentine Church that its art should be a manifestation of true doctrine in the most appropriate form possible. When El Greco arrived in Toledo he was the only painter of calibre in the city. His first big commission came from one of its foremost authorities, the dean of the cathedral, so once his reputation in Toledo was secured by the masterpieces of the '70s it is most probable that he became part of the 'reforming' establishment himself.

Somehow church commissions do not have the prestige now that they had then. To us it is almost unthinkable that so

6 El Greco, *The Burial of Count Orgaz*
Iglesia de San Tome, Toledo, 480 x 360cm

distinguished an artist should have worked closely and willingly with one. Let us suspend our disbelief, and remember that the Church was the repository of knowledge and wisdom, and the creative dynamic of the time. It was quite natural for artists to serve so pre-eminent an institution. While today a paternal arts council watches over the scrupulous examination of our subjectivity, in those days the artist was an adept of beauty, itself an image and radiance of truth. It is difficult for us to understand now how little personality had to do—for them—with the formation of style. Style was not 'the man', but more the accidental mark evolved in the friction between the character of a job to be done and the means available to do it. Rather than search for the originality of El Greco's art in some arresting aspect of his personality, or some putative mysticism, we should better ask what he set out to do. If the Church was involved with his art in such a consultative role, to what extent was he the interpreter of his clients' wishes, or just their illustrator?

As we can see from the writing of Alonso de Orozco,[1] theology was differently conducted in sixteenth century Toledo than in our century. The Church was not under the same cultural pressure to rationalize its explanations, and since the powers of the land partook of its sacraments, its conflict with the State was not a political or ideological one, but simply one of executive roles and legal rights. Theology was conducted seriously and enthusiastically with a view to the person of Christ. The characters of sacred history were examined at all levels—spiritual, analogical and literal— and a new realism about human motives acted as a challenge to exegetes to put sacred history into a convincing perspective. The theology of the time was more a spirituality than a metaphysic or a philosophy of God. At the heart of it the person of Christ was allowed to address in quite realistic terms the person of the reader. Biblical exegesis worked hard to establish the freedom of the sinner by showing just how profound was the condescension of the Father in the gift of his Son, and how generous and authentic was the obedience of the Son in fulfilling the work of the Father. Since this is addressed to a Person rather than a savant or philosopher it is perhaps fair to describe the time as an age of 'ascents' rather than schemas, an age for inner life rather than for explanations. At the heart of Tridentine spirituality was the gasp of wonder at the Father who, through the ineffable gift of his

Son—Love made palpable through the human form divine—
supersedes the Law and makes men heir to his freedom.

El Greco shared the (timeless) apprehensions of his time, and
throughout his life sought to hold in inseparable unity the freedom bequeathed by Love and the palpable form of this gift in
Jesus, God made man. The language of his style is an attempt to
hold the distance traversed by God's condescension in a unity that
will move us by its urgent relevance for our human condition in
three distinct ways. Firstly, the matter of this style has to provide
an opportunity where the devotee of Christ can identify with the
mystery of Divine Love sensuously; where the image of Christ
brings home to men the palpable care of the Father. Secondly,
the drama of the God-Man contract has to be expressed with
classical simplicity in the traditional sacred acts at the heart of the
Church's life. Thirdly, El Greco seeks to make an art where the
soul of the penitent can find an image on which its own transformation may be modelled.

The first matter (the 'palpable' sense of the divine) accounts
for the importance El Greco attached to spontaneity and the sen-
suousness of his forms. If you remember what we said of the
differences between drawing and painting you will notice that El
Greco resists the identifying role implicit in drawing, just for the
acquisitive element that may lurk there. The spontaneity of the
brushwork skates over the form rather than describes it. Even in
his sometimes very realistic portraits the image is experienced
rather than possessed. Things in El Greco's world are to be
enjoyed not for our recognition of them but for their place in a
total cosmos. We have seen how he will alternate within one canvas
between an apparent realism and the artifice he finds proper to
the sacred drama. It is only when we look into this realism that
we discover the brushwork is serving some quite remote dramatic
role in an abstract relation to the whole. What we have enjoyed in
his realism is the human flavour and experience of the detail
rather than a description. Indeed, the relationship between image
and reality, between copy and model, is rendered untraceable, and
the form of the sacred dance subsumes every representation. The
sacred dance itself is impersonal, but made alive by a heightened
personal sensibility. El Greco's insistence on the spontaneity of
any true experience comprises an insistence on the humanity of
the Incarnation which gives the gift of our life back to us
(sensibly, even) with our divinised and transformed humanity.

The second means determining El Greco's style (the lucid and simple exposition of sacred acts) pertains to the contemporary idea of a church itself being a theatre where the sacred event is re-enacted. This is the sphere where every form is immutable, where art partakes in the ceremony of rite. Here the artist is required to be strictly selfless in following the undividedness and purity of a traditional will to form. And, with all the remoteness of El Greco's figures they unerringly record the sacred act required. The figures occupy the full space without distraction and the composition is set by the gestures of the dramatic act. The strange low-relief in which the figures move and have their being alerts us to the autonomy of a heavenly world, a world that has a being other than our own, but a world once entered where the action reads with its own consistency. How different it may be remarked, is this 'classicism' from what we normally understand to be a classical style! This apparent odour of 'difference' I take to have evolved from the tension within the artist's situation between a classical acceptance of the Church's traditional teaching and the reformist needs of the Church in Tridentine times. The reformer is under threat, and the threat forces him to a new self-consciousness. It is this which impels him to cut away the extraneous growth by making a more radical definition of his cause. Such was El Greco's situation confronted by the new skills of verisimilitude that a historical development had forced on an unwary church. His insistence on the involvement of sensibility (hitherto deemed too earthy a category) with the divinization of the human, was an attempt to make specific certain Catholic scruples that had remained silent before the onslaught of new human sciences. The originality of El Greco's solution to a historical dilemma lay not in clinging to an empty form of classical exposition, but in ensuring that the dramatic content that enlivened his new rhetorical language was indeed, Classical, simple and pure. In his best work this proved an inexhaustible source of strength, for, where the followers of Raphael appear as conservatives holding on to forms whose inner meaning and logic became ever more remote as time separates them from their genesis, the challenge of the tension between form and content in El Greco's work keeps it ever contemporary.

The third accomplishment of El Greco's style is the one by which he is most popularly identified, and the one that has suggested to so many its background in mystical experience. This is the powerful visual metaphor of the *figura serpentina* for the flame of penitent desire. This metaphor is never spelt out, it never becomes a symbol, but is left open. Exposed to it without the interference of the conscious intelligence, we experience its extraordinary and troubling power. The perpetual movement of his flame is the sign of inner life, of that potential afforded by the Kingdom within us for an upward and infinite ascent. This movement is like the rise and fall of melody, with a long slow ascent; a break; a rise through a long arc, a turning back and a rise again. In the paintings of full-length saints, sometimes single and sometimes in pairs, this movement is allowed its fullest autonomy, but in the larger paintings on themes central to the Church's teaching this movement is particularized to reinforce the dramatic action. The figures of the Christian drama itself partake of this Christian 'becoming', but discreetly, and never to deprive them of the almost neutral expression that the Mediterranean Christian world deemed appropriate to sacred personae.

These paintings afford us a self-image for the transformation wrought in the soul by conversion. In this El Greco responded to the spirituality of the day, a faith-orientated spirituality. It was faith which prepared the space in the soul where charity might reside—faith which had an 'essential likeness' to God, which is yet only our means to bring about that desirable transformation. If faith is the 'royal way', then the art that celebrates it has to present the world as a concourse, a passage in a two-way contract. Gone, then, is the resplendent vision of a definitive Heaven to which the medievals gave their allegiance; gone, the poised gestures of the Elect. If there is a gesture in El Greco's figures that is specially his creation, (and most of that gesture language can be found in Michelangelo and his followers) it is the gesture of the upraised arm with the palm up-raised. It is the gesture for transmitting grace and its ownership is usually angelic. This figure appears diminutively in the last version of *Christ Driving the Traders out of the Temple*. Entering the 'wrong' side of the painting (that is, on the side of the painting occupied by the Jews who have rejected Christ), the art historian, Rudolf Wittkower showed that here the artist indicates that 'redemption is not just the perogative of those who live in the Faith, but that those siding with evil may be redeemed if they experience an inner conversion.'[2]

In the old Mediterranean world authority and wisdom were seen in the abiding, the still, the image of the Unmoved Mover of the world. True, this stillness had to be a living stillness and, though rarely achieved, it haunted that world, Christian and pagan alike. It is hard to appreciate how radically new El Greco's image of Christian becoming was to the world of the sixteenth century. There is, however, a humanism implicit in his imagery of transformation that immediately sets it apart from the absoluteness of Raphael's Renaissance synthesis. Instead of the Christian being defined by an identity of allegiance, however august it may be, he is, for the first time, defined by his pilgrim nature. Conversion is seen to be what it is, sans termination. Modern man who recognizes in the disestablishment of the Christian the sign of his authentic allegiance to a kingdom not of his world, is much more ready to accept the religious category symbolized by the pilgrim than any other.

At this point I hear my reader with well-intentioned scepticism enquire, 'And did El Greco consciously decide to paint this way to fulfil the programme you have described?' to which I can only reply—'Substantially, yes!' What convinces me, against all the romantic allegiance of my youth, is the intellectual passion present in his apprehension of form. The world that first greets us from the various paintings that comprised the San Domingo el Antiguo altarpiece is so rigorously consistent, so poised and confident in its marriage of bold conception with brilliant handling, that we can only say, 'Here is a mind in possession of itself.' Doubtless El Greco did not sit down and programme a specification for a required form of painting. There must have been some inspiration in which all the loose impressions, the disconnected scents that he picked up from his contemporaries, suddenly made a new whole. In some intuition he must have coalesced a ground where all those intellectual difficulties that were such a problem to the successors of Michaelangelo could be held together in a meaningful way. He did, after all, have the great man's example before him to prove the equality of painting with the arts of the word. Of all the Italians, Michelangelo was the closest to him spiritually, and he had the great advantage of discovering him from a Greek background. In his second exile he would recreate Michelangelo after the practice and craft of the Venetian colourists, according to the new and vivid lights of Counter-Reformation theology.

II

We have seen from the foregoing that if El Greco can be called a visionary painter it is not because he dressed in sackcloth and lived an obscure life in an upper room having visions. The ignorant would turn every painter into a 'recorder' and, while recording what the camera records presents them with no problems, they imagine that the man who paints 'out of his head' is essentially doing the same thing: copying an image there. But, of course, both the realist and the so called 'visionary' are involved in very complex artifices of creating a 'seeming' out of coloured mud from something that already has a quite incomparable existence whether materially or inwardly. They are only concerned that the seeming 'works', that it is 'convincing'. The success of this has nothing to do with copying, but with the analogies that can be found between the 'unlike' or with the appropriatenesses that may be found between ways of working and the work that may be completed.

We know from the record of Pacheco's visit to the ageing artist that El Greco was a 'bit of a philosopher'. He wrote a treatise on architecture and another on painting, and though, unfortunately, these are lost, recently his own copy of Vitruvius' *On Architecture* has come to light with quite extensive annotations in his own hand. Two quotations may be helpful if we can allow for the formality and courtesy of sixteenth-century language:

> Painting is the only thing that can judge everything else . . . (it) occupies the position of prudent moderator of all that is visible.

> Painting, because of its universality, becomes speculative and never lacks substance to speculate on . . .

Painting acting as a 'prudent moderator', joining things that in nature seem separate. Why do we need things to be 'joined'? What is the separateness that threatens unity or universality? The 'prudent moderator' suggests one who brings the claims of rival factions (or faculties?) around a conference table, it would seem that something in our carnal nature 'separates', whereas, in a word, it is imagination which allows different faculties to be, as it were, represented in the one image.

The 'speculation' of this image making 'moderatorship' would seem an incomparably different way of knowing than by an act of the discursive intelligence. Intelligence rules by division, by identifying and comparing: it presupposes a subject to which it establishes an objective relation. The 'speculation' of this (should we call it?) intuition cannot be too busy. I believe we would be quite entitled to find in the activity of the discursive intellect a certain cruelty. The intellect divides us from what we know and divides what we know from its brothers by making it an object the better to describe it. The more rigorously the intellect scrutinises the object the more the object evades the person of the knower. Intellect is masculine: intellect strides on the high steps of dialectic. Meanwhile imagination gathers what is known among the personal faculties of the knower. Imagination is feminine and acts receptively to the transcendence of the 'idea' casting a web among the faculties so that the imperial inner realm may get a delicate and shining concreteness. Imagination may be tempted—what 'immanence' is not subject to temptation?—but, guided by a pure heat, it has the power to find forms, through an exactly felt system of correspondence and analogy, through the precision of its omissions as much as the inclusiveness of its faculties, that are an equivalent of any fact or state of being that may exist. Facts of nature may be more or less comforting or pleasing to see expressed in corresponding form, but 'states of being'? They are the unique prerogative of the imaginative act. It is imagination that relates the 'inner' to the 'outer'; it is imagination that gathers our life into a new whole and throws it at some 'overwhelming question'.

The classical world was sanguine about imagination. From Plato on it was generally regarded as a function of the lower soul dependent upon sense perceptions from which the soul must purify itself. The only word Antiquity had to describe imagination was *phantasia* which translates for us as that ignominious Walter Mitty-like faculty wherein our wish fulfilment takes over. Plato, whose noble and curious heart was almost equally divided between the poet and the idealist within him, was anxious, and therefore unremittingly harsh, about the dangers of the poetic imagination. Christian clerics for their part were not slow in quoting Plato to keep art in its place—the market place of illusion. The archbishop who was contemporary with El Greco in Toledo, Gaspar de Quiroga, was a reformer in the Tridentine mould and the first thing he did on assuming office was to ban mime and drama from the cathedral. However, he did not ban El Greco. May we not here recognise the great 'and yet . . .' that floats suspended—and continues to float—over the question of the artistic imagination? This 'and yet . . .' represents the universal consensus that, in practice, imagination cannot be adequately described as 'fantasy', and that some art has always had the task of 'raising the spirit', and of saying things that the most elevated intellectual discourse can only approach quite clumsily.

We do not understand the way the spirit works in the vehicle that nature offers it, and, possibly it is salutary that we cannot. Imagination is such a vehicle, and perhaps a certain unknowing is the one guarantee that it needs for its essential secrecy. History again and again reveals that, without grace in our hearts, the human faculties heap up jealously against each other just like the rest of us. An artist may be forgiven for pointing out that the intellect is no exception.

Despite the lowliness that the philosophers of Antiquity ascribed to imagination one exceptional voice defended it. Plotinus still takes intellection as the appropriate means to knowledge, but he does allow that imagination can arrive at 'equivalents'. To the question of whether imagination is involved in mental acts, he answers:

> If in fact every mental act is accompanied by an image, we may well believe that when this image, which would be as it were a picture of the thought, remains on, this explains how an object of knowledge takes place. But if this is not the case another suggestion may be made. Perhaps memory would be the reception into the imagination of the discursive sequel (logos) to an act of the intuitive thought (noêma). The thought itself being indivisible and never, as it were, rising to the exterior of consciousness, remains hidden within, but the logos, unfolding and proceeding from the thought into the imagination, displays the thought as in a mirror. . .[3]

In other words, the images that imagination makes can reflect an intellectual content.

Plotinus hardly credited imagination with the capability for a 'pure intellectual act' but conceded the ability of an interior image to mirror such an act for the soul.[4] The soul had to be calm and likened to the sky-reflecting waters of a lake: in that state it had a transcendental orientation. The imagination for Plotinus represented the mid point of the soul's life. This led him to conceive it as Janus-faced with its upper limit bordering on the life of the intellect and its lower limit bordering on the senses. He vacillates between identifying imagination as one faculty facing in two directions, or as two faculties, a higher and a lower imagination. In this latter case he allows that the two faculties may, in certain propitious circumstances, work together, the light of the lower, as he puts it, being absorbed in the light of the higher. This anticipates across the ages the English nineteenth-century poet, Coleridge, who never tired of reminding his countrymen that 'imaginative fantasy' was a contradiction in terms. Coleridge held that fantasy makes images for our personal desires which so rudely experience the limits of impersonal nature; it acts on the level of nature for the advantage of the Self, cossetting it against its little deaths. Imagination (Plotinus' 'higher faculty') creates images which gather the disparate faculties of the soul in the experience of a universal apperception, enabling the mind to contemplate new wholes between the duality of spirit and nature. There are those, of course, who argue that there is no duality between spirit and nature. Artists abhor their claim because, if they have any sense, they realize imagination has been made redundant.

Iambilicus (at about the same time as Plotinus) knew the difficult 'apartness' of the intellect, its need for the watering of the imagination. In *De Mysteriis* he wrote about that branch of divination known as 'drawing down the light', which

> illuminates the aethereal and luminous vehicle of the real with divine light, so that divine images take hold of our imagination, stimulated by the will of the gods. For the whole life of the soul and all the faculties in it are subject to the gods and moved by them in accordance with the wish of the conductors.[5]

The 'conductor' (of the light) does not lose consciousness: imagination just receives an extra dimension. He goes on to point out how the divine light by-passes the discursive consciousness on its way to the imagination, because that consciousness would, as he puts it, 'interpose a degree of self-consciousness.'

Most of the philosophers following Plotinus (though obviously not Porphyry or Iambilicus) reverted to Plato's anathema against imagination. An academic idealism is a much safer place for an intellectual to reside, because any sort of 'drawing down of light' requires spiritual discernment . . . and who can be trusted with that! Nevertheless Plotinus remained one of the most influential philosophers coming up to El Greco's time, Michelangelo drawing much comfort from him.

If things were as Plotinus said, and natural phenomena were the unreliable imitation of an 'idea', and if God's face was necessarily withdrawn and invisible, in between were, nevertheless, all the 'correspondences' which imagination might divine between these elusive extremities. Should an artist choose to represent the god he must have the mind to conceive an effective 'as if'. 'Phidias,' says Plotinus, 'wrought the Zeus in Olympia upon no model of things of sense, but by approaching what form Zeus might take if he chose to become manifest to sight.' In other words, the artist must have sufficient taste for heavenly things to know what might be involved for a god in a certain godly choice.

If we may summarise our discussion about imagination it would seem to be in the seat of power for three major activities. First, it relates the inner and the outer, personalising a world that otherwise would be totally alien, allowing nature to be, at times, an epiphany for man.

Secondly, it relates the senses with the intellect, thus humanising the bodily faculties so that they can partake of or reflect the choices of the soul.

Finally, it relates the ultimately possible to the necessary so that our hearts are not crushed by the limitations of finitude, mortality and the malice of the world.

On the credit of this perhaps we may say that visionary art is an act, not of the practical will, but of the will acting for the spirit as a whole. That, I believe, is how El Greco saw it.

The visionary artist of today works out of himself. By the nature of the materialist society in which we find ourselves his work necessarily carries a heightened aura of the spiritual, but quite possibly stems from a personal fantasy made respectable by good taste. The artist will surely be quite incapable of discussing it with anyone, or benefiting from the structures of tradition in the widest sense of the word. Such was the community of intuition at El

Greco's time that not only could he make a visionary art, but he could discuss it, adapt it to the occasion that arose, plan it so that it could fulfil a required intelligible programme, design and make the frames to contain it—and still not feel demeaned by having so many 'non-artistic' claims made upon his attention!

But if the vision of imagination was an act, as we have suggested, then it was primarily an act of service. When we study any of the larger projects of El Greco's career we find there an elaborate chain of purposes. These purposes were discussed over long periods and the evidence is that he treated them with the utmost professional respect. Such a commission comprised the three late paintings he did for the Tavera Hospital. Since the hospital was to be dedicated to St John the Baptist the artist was asked to make three retables on the theme of rebirth. Discussions began as early as 1595, but it was not until 1608 that a scheme was finally agreed upon.

The patron of El Greco's last great schema in Toledo was the administrator of the hospital, Pedro Salazar de Mendoza. Salazar was an able and humane administrator and also a respected ecclesiastical scholar devoted to maintaining the prestige of the city. His chief preoccupation at the time was the rehabilitation of the late archbishop Carrenza. Carrenza had in 1559 suffered imprisonment by the authorities of the Inquisition, and had after many years of exile been pardoned, but was never fully cleared of the charges laid against him. The archbishop had been popular and respected for his piety so the whole episode was a very unhappy one for the Toledan church. Salazar wrote a biography in vindication of Carrenza, so what more natural consequence but to employ a painter to exemplify the theology of the deceased archbishop 'because painting,' he said, 'stirs and elevates the spirit more than writing.'

The theme of 'rebirth' finally agreed was to underline the triumph of the Christian life over the world and time (with, in this case, its injustices). The three events chosen for the retables were the Annunciation (or as the Spanish church of the time liked to call it, the Incarnation), the Baptism of Christ, and the Revelation of St John the Evangelist. Unfortunately the scheme was dogged by prevarication and disaster and at the time of the contract El Greco only had six more years to live. The first and last works of the contract were incomplete at his death, and it took Jorge

Manuel another ten years of haggling with the hospital authorities before they were handed over. By that time Salazar had moved to another position, so a different taste arranged that a different artist be engaged to complete the work. While the great *Baptism* has always hung in the hospital the original placement of the works was never adhered to.

The most remarkable and haunting of the three paintings is *The Vision of St John the Evangelist* now in the Metropolitan Museum of New York. The iconography of this work is still a matter of dispute. Originally Cossio identified its theme as the Opening of the Fifth Seal from the ninth chapter of the Apocalypse. Recently, however, Richard Mann[6] has argued for its interpretation as the Resurrection of the Just (fig. 7). Much of Carrenza's theology was absorbed with St John's vision of the end of time, so it is highly probable that Salazar would have chosen this theme in vindication of the unjustly accused archbishop, hoping that one day heaven's judgement would upturn the verdict of misguided men. The imagery of the translucent bodies corresponds to Carrenza's description of the four graces which will characterise the Just in heaven—spirituality, lightness, radiance and freedom from pain. The mysterious draperies that envelop the Just, to which they do not seem to have truly accustomed themselves, likewise stem from Carrenza's description. Endorsing St Paul's imagery of putting on the new imperishable garments of immortality, Carrenza was emphatic that this heavenly clothing would not be needed to cover the body, or protect it against the elements. Its sole purpose would be to mark the glorious state of the Elect. The little *putti* who with such unworldly grace donate clothing to the Just are the souls of the Just who have come to inhabit their resurrected bodies. Salazar's own writings make the distinction between the properties of bodies subject to death and souls which exist eternally. Salazar was offended by most pictures of the resurrection because they did not show the reunion of souls with bodies.

With this imagery we find ourselves floating in a complex double metaphor for embodiment. Here El Greco holds a unique position among artists of his day in giving a quite literal theological transcription. How unlike the Elect in any other Christian representation are these Just who wait at the confines of heaven! Obedient this imagery may be to Carrenza's theology, but every component of it has been recreated from the inside. The immense St John bears

7 El Greco, *Resurrection of the Elect*
Metropolitan Museum of Art, New York, 225 x 193cm

no relation to any vision-receiving saint in art. He is not beholden to a vision that stays outside him: he is 'rapt", as consumed in God as was that other St John who wrote the *Ascent of Mount Carmel*. The figure of the saint and the souls of the Just who are the object of his vision are totally devoid of pious or cultural rhetoric; quite without reference to anything we comfortably know, except our Christian hope. Here at last is a completely fluid world where all divisions have been superseded and the artist, the saint and the Just share the same ecstatic 'being' before God.

It must be acknowledged, however, that this strange painting, acting on the borders of death and eternity, is unfinished. Perhaps the painting was unfinishable and, if so, we must be grateful to Jorg Manuel for leaving his father's work untampered with. There are some ambiguities in colour: why should so commanding a figure be in so passive a colour as blue-grey? Rather than any further development of the image, the painting surely awaited a few final glazes.

In the *Celestial Hierarchies* of the Pseudo Dionysius (which El Greco had on his bookshelf) we find an exposition of the 'dis-similar similitudes' by which the soul may be prevailed to rise to God. The soul, the philosopher believed, rose by the 'similar', but since the similar ultimately had no similarity (was, perhaps, only an idealisation?), the dissimilar might at times be more appropriate. Since both Dionysius and Plotinus were philosophers of the same school and both interested in 'light' and its symbolism, it is quite likely that El Greco was acquainted with a spiritual exercise that Plotinus[7] enumerated in his *Tractates* to bring alive his points of doctrine. It is, in a certain sense, an exercise in embodiment:

> Imagine a small luminous mass serving as centre to a trans-parent sphere, so that the light within shows on the entire outer surface, otherwise unlit: we surely agree that the inner core of light, intact and immobile reaches out over the entire outer extension; the simple light of that small centre illu-minates the whole field. The diffused light is not due to any bodily magnitude of that central point which illuminates not as a body, but as body lit, that is by another kind of power than corporeal quality; let us then abstract the corporeal mass, retaining the light as power: we can no longer speak of the light in any particular spot; it is equally diffused within and

throughout the entire sphere. We can no longer name the spot it occupied so as to say whence it came or how it is present; we can but seek and wonder as the search shows us the light simultaneously present at each and every point of the sphere.

(trans. Stephen McKenna)[8]

The similarity of the spiritualization proposed[9] by this exercise to the spiritualization offered in the paintings of El Greco is surely striking. If we take the artist's brushwork corresponding to the living flame as the means by which we share his experience (sensuously, as it were), he then, under our nose, deprives that sensibility of the reference we would expect to substantiate it, and fills that emptiness with the content of his spiritual contemplation.

This is not some magic, but a discipline in which the 'speculation' of imagination is purged of any subjectivity. It is a method of meditation whose classical source, I believe, should not unduly worry us. El Greco here is using a procedure of meditation on a totally Christian content under the eye of the reforming Church. It is worth noting that, according to Louis Marx in his book, *The Poetry of Meditation*, one period when such meditation flourished coincides exactly with the zenith of English religious poetry. Talking about the poet George Herbert, T.S. Eliot says,[10]

> All poetry is difficult, almost impossible, to write: and one of the great permanent causes of error in writing poetry is the difficulty of distinguishing between what one really feels and what one would like to feel, and between the moments of genuine feeling and the moments of falsity. This is the danger of all poetry: but it is a peculiarly grave danger in the writing of devotional verse.

Personally I prefer the description 'religious' to 'devotional', since devotion, however 'lifted' its object, is always from a self. But a special benefit of meditation may well be that it secures the art—whether painting or poetry—from the sort of self-consciousness that later religious expressions in all forms fell prey to.

The underlying theme of all El Greco's work is embodiment, the embodiment of what cannot be embodied, that which the Catholic Church names sacramentally in the expression, 'Corpus

Christi'. His importance to Christians as an artist lies not in his style, or even in the audacity of his solution to a 'reformist' art, but in his quest of the appropriate metaphor for an embodiment of the sacred, a true 'manifestation'. The human race, Christians believe, stands indebted to the embodiment of God in the Son. This vital doctrine of the Tridentine Church was used by some to justify the degree of naturalism employed by the artists of the Renaissance. In that embodiment rest so many possibilities of grace—for us. If the Son's body was the temple of the Holy Spirit, ours may be the same. El Greco saw, however, the egotism that attaches to bodies and developed his art to anticipate the pantheism of our relish in the identification of holy and natural conjoinings. He saw his contemporaries treat the Incarnate One as a hero and realised that this was the height of Humanism's comprehension of the Son's sacredness. El Greco, like the iconographers of his original homeland saw the Son, not as a hero, but as the sacred manifestation to men. That manifestation became the model of his art. That is why he insists in his paintings on the inviolable nature of Christ's flesh. It is to reinforce the distinctness of the sacred that he creates a disembodied world in honour of embodiment.

VII

IN PRAISE OF SOLITUDE

When we come to the matter of cultural or artistic loyalties we reach the most intractable core of human identity. As we saw in Chapter V, the dethronement of Raphael was less thinkable than the unseating of any European monarch in the last five hundred years. Nevertheless the nineteenth century gradually emptied this identity of its living heart, and the war of 1914 finally shattered the kingdom of which he was arbiter. I have suggested (from the safety of those intervening years) that he reigned by default, but so many hopes and identities were invested in Raphael that what can be said now with impunity was unsayable only one hundred and fifty years ago. The halftruths by which a civilization continues are things that we have to be very careful of.

There is a sense in which Christian civilization is a liability for Christianity. The civilization half has a way of dragging down the Christianity. The root of Christianity has a way of being rendered mute, while the civilization part careers off in all manner of enchanting directions. As we have seen, the art-historical developments of the sixteenth and seventeenth centuries were witness to a whole series of short cuts and accommodations made between the institutions of Christianity and the social needs as they were perceived at the time. The Evangelicals (those who saw the cause of the Counter-Reformation in the most black and white terms) won over those who saw the relation of the Church's voice to our temporal needs in more perennial terms. Today's theological answers proved themselves to be the next generation's stumbling block.

The myriad constellation of acts that makes a civilization creates a taste, but when that civilization loses the true sense of its own roots it develops contradictions without having the energy to resolve them. This is what happened to Christian civilization. Taste wells up from some instinctive region where the residue of our acts has already recast the symbols appropriate to them. At the centre of the constant pull between decay and renewal taste acts as the modest handmaid who witnesses all. In comparing the Byzantines and Raphael with El Greco we have seen how in certain ways the symbols of Christianity stayed the same and yet were emptied or recharged with unique appropriateness.

How trumpery were the evidences of Protestant taste when I was growing up—its coy domesticity, its moral blackmail with humility! Catholic taste was so awful that it caused a sort of cleansing amazement; the lie of its unction was so preposterous as to be a lie on the grand scale. And while it is hard to trace the deterioration of Anglo-Protestant taste to any artist whose name has survived in the history books, the deformation of Catholic taste goes back to some quite famous artists, depending on how radically you view that deterioration. The noble rhetoric of Raphael proved more susceptible to time than Pope Julius II could have suspected. The first casualty to its authority was the excesses of the Baroque. Men, even then, were too stage-struck to resist peopling their proud new spaces (the offspring of their new building techniques) with a Disneyland of saints and virtues whose real meaning they had forgotten. We may concede to the Baroque the vitality of a good floor show, but what can be said of Murillo? Here Raphael's synthesis is padded out in cotton wool and served up with the gravy of an ersatz sentiment. Out of a twilight space the rheumy eyes of God appeal, bereft.

No wonder the Moderns felt such a sense of mission to clean up the metaphysical mess left by the bad habits of Christianity!

It would seem retrospectively very unfortunate for Christianity that after the medieval period theology was unable to sustain a Christian aesthetic of the beautiful. Taste became associated with the effeminate and the worldly, and the serious concerns of theology moved to moral and intellectual justification. In the theology of El Greco's contemporaries the aesthetic still had a foothold in its thought for personal development. It was accepted that the person must change in one way or another, and that this transformation was allpervasive, while yet, in this life, incomplete. Here was the region where the aesthetic was irrevocably tied to value. When I was young I was happy to take pleasure in sentimental pictures, or stimulating grandiosities. Now I am older I need not gape at such things.

Perhaps a certain Christian stoicism or puritanism actually ends up more worldly than common sense allows. If the 'Good Fight' is taken too literally or applied too directly to the contexts of the world the heart ends up cramped and closed with unlived life. Perhaps a certain inheritance from Scholasticism has stamped us with an 'angelism': because of the intellect's likeness to God we must be seen to make our conscious mind our master. We forget that intelligence is more than consciousness, and this has caused great barrenness where there should have been riches and gifts. Taste *is* a part of our knowing. Its absence *is* found to substantiate a lack of judgment. If this soft, apparently passive, area is not acknowledged, if a free area is not encouraged where imagination and sensibility can rearrange the world as part of their own unfolding, then will and intelligence are left cold and unmodified by the affective life. This has been fateful in the life of the Church. By neglecting the aesthetic sphere the Church has lost, in matters of taste, its discernment of spirits.

My intention is not to make lament for an Age of Faith, for I recognize that we must accept history, warts and all. I do not believe, however, that this acceptance commits us to a comparative or relativist view of history in which each age's commitment to truth is a comparable counter with every other age's. It is, I believe, dishonest to make oneself a spectator and treat the passing of history as a story for the judgment of an omnipotent present. Every age has the right to as personal a biography as a human person has. If Christian civilization was betrayed from within that is a tragedy, another story in which the Cross is mirrored, a sobering failure that can leaven our hearts of their vanity.

II

From the faithful's diet of lachrymose rhetoric provided by El Greco's successors to the analytical naturalism of the Impressionists, European painting pursued its remarkably consistent course on a metalled way. The Counter-Reformation was the last historical movement whence the Church wielded an influence over the artist's imagery. Working for his new patrons amongst the aristocracy and at court, the artist found freedom to follow his intricate pursuit of verisimilitude whither it might take him. There were exceptions, like William Blake, who stood very much to the side of this route, but they were hardy individualists whom the now vulnerable imagery and mythos of the Church could not assist. Odd to relate, no sooner was the metalled way consummated, through that elegant lucidity of the French mind, in the discoveries of the Impressionists, than it was seen to be a trap. Instead of this insight of objectivity providing for painters a method, immediately Gauguin, Seurat, Cezanne and countless others opened a critique of Impressionism, its superficiality, its materialism and its unyieldingness to further developments. Was that metalled road not a bright temptation, a peculiar destiny that Europe had to suffer; its denouement at the point of Impressionism comprising the birth of our contemporary selfconsciousness, our anxiety and the self-distrust with which ever since our life has been spiced?

> Enjoyed no sooner but despised straight,
> Past reason hunted, and no sooner had,
> Past reason hated as a swallowed bait. . . .

It was at this juncture people started to look at El Greco again. Suddenly the Renaissance did not seem such an unmitigated boon as it had seemed to our Victorian great-grandfathers. With cheap photographic reproduction and universal education the whole history of art looked quite different. Archaic styles that the Victorians had dismissed as barbaric became repositories of artistic and spiritual good sense. With the reappraisal of the Renaissance, suddenly El Greco changed from being a villain to being a hero.

The modern sensibility is, in thought, solitary; perhaps infernally solitary. This sensibility is absorbed with the nakedness and vulnerability of the individual encompassed by the meaninglessness of reality. He must be brave and take the medicine of a deepening disillusion. Beauty and honour, which for Christian man point to the transcendent, are ever more unobtainably shelved away by a historial determinism that can only recognize the quantifiable. With Christianity man is the embodiment of a heavenly promise: without it the individual is reduced to a shivering nerve end. Self-consciousness perfects this nerve end with a wonderful resilience and solitude polishes this resilience into pride.

The position of El Greco in relation to the art of our time has, I believe, a more than coincidental similarity to the position of Kierkegaard's philosophy to the thought of our contemporaries. Both were committed Christians who thought through their

Christianity. Both were anxious to keep up the price of Christianity by manifesting the reality of its categories for the individual. But it was the uncompromisingness that their solitude visited on their thought, the peculiar depth at which the perennial human condition is submitted to the fire of enquiry that speaks to our generations across the centuries. Both men were in that profoundly modern situation of remaking the discipline of their work from the ground up to suit their special purposes. The Modern rejects the beneficent consolation of faith that is the occasion of his need, but the intuitions of the need in themselves (and as given us by these two Christian spokesmen) are fascinating to him.

Over two hundred years and the whole span of continental Europe separate Soren Kierkegaard from El Greco, not to say the intractable differences of the philosopher's craft from the painter's. Ultimately a comparison between them may not be very yielding, but in one way we might notice El Greco's better fortune. The solitude of El Greco is always within the community of the Church. He borrows from the great and the unknown of his age, he enjoys the confidence of his Toledan peers, he is convivial when the occasion calls for it. His solitude does not break the solidarity of the Church. The painter's solitude and the community shape each other. The pursuit of his solitude bears no resentment or malice, implies no exclusion.

A civilization that does not have a place for solitude is brutish. Not the wretched solitude of the typist who 'lays out her camisoles and stays' in a city apartment, not the solitude of the city's hum, but the solitude of desert places, of retreats or mountain chapels. Man is born for community, but he is not able for it without solitude. Every man begins with himself. Every act is witness to a choice, voluntary or involuntary, made by an 'I' that has to be lived with. Every act is witness to the state of being in which the act is grounded. Contemplation alone waters that being. Education helps, but the field needing to be watered is not academic; it is us. Since each one of us is his own first friend, a certain solitude is very space for our souls.

An indigenous people who have not been exploited by others with a superior technology are incapable of what we call 'bad taste'. This is because language has not differentiated the categories of the individual and the group, and the people remain innocent of the myriad self-deceits that accompany such a programme. Their 'contemplation' will be rudimentary because it will not be under the pressure of all those differentiations. The innocence of the unity of being out of which their acts emerge assures the purity of the creative act however utilitarian or metaphysical it may be. Their sacred art is uncloying because it is direct: their utilitarian arts partake of the same poetic as their sacred arts. They are innocent of all those fraught complicities that bind more complex societies together, that hypocrisy which is 'mediocrity's frail tribute to virtue'.

I do not propose that the answer to civilization's ills is for us all to become like Bushmen. 'Sacred' and 'secular' are refined concepts that bring with them a deeper and more complex responsibility: grown-up gods are more exacting than infantile ones. But the more complex the distinctions that language creates, the more solitude we need to reconcile these distinctions within ourselves. Language is like the Promethean fire, the 'given' that comes from the gods. Much as we may regret it, the gods from whom the fire descends are not all equal: they, at least, are incomparably themselves! Primitive societies do not recognize the need for solitude—except, significantly, for their priests and shamans, the bearers of language, and therefore of distinctions. The tribe is gregarious, because the personality is undefined.

In Toledo solitude was respected because of the ineffable distance between God and his creature. The community recognized that everyone is alone in his experience of that distance. We may experience the benignity of that distance as it is willed by the Father's love, or the scandal of it in his Son, in which scandal we participate. Our Book tells us that we each carry the Kingdom of God within us. This is the potential and guarantee of our humanity. That was the 'humanism' of the Church in Toledo: that humanity is the place where God makes himself again. So long as priests (or any other type of shaman) utter this straight and without inversion we have no reason to be afraid of them. Their solitude and ours is the same. Temptation, of course, is always a possibility: but then everybody knows, in the solitude of his chamber, precisely what the score is.

Maybe somebody will one day draw up an epistemology of solitude. The story of art would be one of its best sources. The practice of the old iconographers proposes this solitude having its being through the community of the Christian liturgy. Reform movements propose it through penance and meditation. Agnosticism proposes it through 'truth to self', and Picasso through the flailing of the self in a broken heritage. Solitude is an uncomfortable place for modern man because it is a hall of mirrors.

A Christian epistemology of solitude would be soberly unflattering about what goes on in civilization, realistic in its treatment of its benefits, of the delights of culture. Man in solitude does not save time by gadgets, or develop by the range of his freedoms. In solitude man's acts have to be reconciled with their means. His techniques have to be reconciled to the imperium that is appropriate to him, his culture to the beast behind its mask.

We say that, 'To understand is to forgive.' In civilised society that is specially true. There every man is wise to the labyrinth of adjustments we are each required to perform. Only solitude can bring those adjustments before the court of the spirit's ultimate simplicity. The Self hides in the complicity of its labyrinthine involvements, but in solitude before God there can be no deception. In that solitude every step a man takes forward has to be substantiated by two real steps backwards to recover from the egotism lurking in the forward motion.

If, as may be, only an 'epistemology of solitude' is equipped to know the truth of any act, the discrimination of taste is the instinctive guide that first alerts the inner conscience to make that epistemology.

VIII

THE TIME GATHERER

I

In the plurality of periods and styles encouraged by the 'museum without walls',[1] the healthy sceptic forms his taste in accordance with his perceptions and his sensibility. The formation of taste for the Christian, however, is rather more complex. For him artistic taste will depend on vision—a vision which must, to some extent, be inner vision. The authenticity of this vision will depend on the accuracy and delicacy of a complex series of correspondences—correspondences between the symbols his taste is disposed to, and the way they are used. Taste is no absolute. It offers no hard and fast guide to which we can appeal. Taste is simply the developed habit of good judgment regarding the chain of appropriatenesses in which sensibility and imagination are involved. It could be called a 'common sense of the aesthetic', except that for the Christian it is irrevocably bound up with the vitality of symbols. What Modernity did was to loosen taste from the thraldom of symbols. Hence the tremendous prestige of abstraction as an area where symbolism can be neutralised and, as it were, depoliticised. All that twilight sentiment into which Christianity had allowed its symbols to fall had to be cleared away for hygienic reasons. Modern taste is concerned with the good ordering of sensibility and the psychology of perception. Its field of appropriatenesses is deliberately restricted. The contemporary artist deploys his taste in specialised spheres from which more general and human concerns have conspicuously exited. Significantly when symbols do surface in modern art they tend to emerge negatively as symbols of outrage or despair. There is no use for our contemporaries to tell the Christian that taste in art is all one, and that he does not have it. He knows that taste is an aspect of the instinctive will in whose transformation he is involved. No hygiene can hold him back from the rough and tumble into which his symbolic language precipitates him. However much the Christian may learn from modern art (and there is much he can), his problems in exercising taste prevent him from belonging to 'modernity'.

With a certain reluctance then, I believe we have to admit two contrasting modes, the Christian and the Modern. Contemporary theology may use the most sophisticated casuistry to reconcile them, but if we take seriously the antipodes disclosed in the covert activities of taste we learn more clearly the heights and depths in which the human heart is involved. Artists are not able to negotiate these antipodes with the ideal dispassion of intellectual concepts. They are only able to traverse them through the transactions of taste. Taste may develop and learn to enjoy the 'less' that is 'more', but only after the will and being of the artist himself have been modified.

If we must consult El Greco's Christianity out of our scruple in examining that disjunction of taste I perceive across the ages, there remains one major doubt to be resolved. This must be the question whether, if the artist could be so misread over the ages, and by his heterodox rediscoverers in the nineteenth century, was he not culpable of leaving open the syntax of his symbolic language to allow such diverse interpretations? Is it possible his discipline of meditation and symbolic concurrence was more aesthetic than something so spiritually creditable should really be?

The wise artist is one whose symbolic language is at one with the content of his work; the 'closure' of whose symbols is sufficient to make us suspend our own seeing in preference for another's, but the 'openness' of whose symbols holds them above our everyday trivia and gives future generations the space for movement for the spirit within them. Historical periods are indeed the victims of their prejudices, and art demonstrates, to the chagrin of the prim, that there is no seeing without the prejudice of a strong identity. Every historical period has its own physiological and psychological constitution. Every historical period relates in its own way to the perennial conditions of being human. And no doubt we may say that every period is in some disrelationship with those given conditions . . . and there, perhaps, is the pain out of which poetry is made. El Greco's contemporaries undoubtedly saw his works differently from the way they were seen by the founding fathers of Modernism. They would have been more inclined to see through the materiality of the paint than we do. The rhetorical aspect of the figures would have had much more differentiation than for us, for whom small variations of gesture are reduced to a stylistic element. For them this rhetoric would have been bedded in a whole contract of current manners. The language of religious gesture, the hands of the Virgin in the different scenes from her life, would have been much more evocative for them than we, with our remoteness from the language of liturgy, can easily imagine.

To overcome these barriers it may be helpful to compare El Greco's *Pentecost* in the Prado[2] with a *Pentecost* (pl. 8) painted by a Novgorodian iconographer in fifteenth century Russia.

The icon shows the twelve apostles (Judas excluded and St Paul substituted for him) sitting in a semicircle in a diversified and living harmony. At the summit of the group is a space where the absent One, Christ, would have presided. There is no dove, no Blessed Virgin, there are no visitors to Jerusalem from Asia Minor, no roaring sounds or general perturbation. At the bottom enclosed by a doorway is a representation of the 'peoples' who awaited 'a great light' in the form of a king, worldly, surrounded by the night, who holds on a white cloth the scrolls of the twelve apostles. Being the work of an iconographer the image is the same as countless other 'Pentecosts' done over some hundreds of years.

The iconographer has regarded the historical event at Jerusalem, described in *Acts*, with peremptory dismissal. Instead of that scene of confusion and babble we are given a spiritual description of Pentecost as the historical antithesis to the Tower of Babel, when mankind lost its unity of tongues. Where the uninitiated who witnessed Pentecost thought that the disciples were 'full of new wine', the initiated for whom this icon is intended are shown the true state of affairs—that the Bride of Christ is set on earth, that the Spirit presides in the diverse gifts of the faithful, and that in the freedom of Christ the Church has the grace to speak in one language, at least metaphorically, in the unity of love.

The symbolism of the icon is a coded mystery. Not comprehending it I find it beautiful and solemn: comprehending it I find it much more moving. I acknowledge a mystery of the Church in fixed form. I do not want it to be any other way. It contains the potentiality of correspondence to my Christian experience which will be filled out in my own destiny whatever that may be.

El Greco's *Pentecost* (pl. 8) allows a literal interpretation of the historical event without pressing on the spectator a carnal or uninitiated vision of it. In this sense it is simpler to read than the icon, for it reads as a single image. Everything in the icon is described through a conceptual analogy: with El Greco's painting the freedom in the symbols from conceptual definition encourages us to share in the experience, an exaltation in the Church's confirmation from above. The other profound difference between the representations is the presence of the Blessed Virgin at the centre, a distinction which we may attribute to Orthodox and Catholic traditions. As Orthodox and Catholic teaching concur on the importance of our Lady I can only think her absence in the icon is due to a need to present the corporate Church. In both traditions, as well as having her special relationship with her Son, she is the mother of the Church, and therefore our mother. Her presence at the heart of El Greco's painting is what allows the painter to unify the group and maintain the momentum of excitement in the flickering low relief of the drapery which seems to hang from the delicate row of heads that cross the top of the painting.

In El Greco nothing is 'fixed'; everything, typically, is described in the melting pot of a spiritual 'becoming'. My disbelief is suspended by the rhetoric of an experience I am forced to recognise. I know that the apostles in the painting are not 'drunk with new wine', but are partaking in the 'becoming' of the Church initiated with Pentecost. Even sharing in this becoming I share in the Being who encompasses that becoming. El Greco's art does not maintain the remoteness of the coded mysterious art of the iconographer. It is an art, rather, that addresses me personally in my anxiety and longing. And it must be so since I know that in this creaturely centre of myself I can waver. And thus, reaching, as it does, the source of my most tender anxiety, the descending grace of God's spirit demonstrated by El Greco's *Pentecost* transforms me.

So much does El Greco insist on addressing me as an individual offering me an experience, that I can easily be misled to think that the structure of a literal event is not there. That, however, was El Greco's ultimate achievement—to describe the

8 El Greco, *Christ Healing the Blind Man*
Galleria Nazionale, Parma, 50 x 61cm

sacred events in the highly readable way that the Church required as 'message', so that doctrine is done justice to, while at the same time communicating these doctrines through a shared experience that has that quality of surprise that experience so often has. How does the poet restore the extraordinary to the everyday?

El Greco was always the master of the poet's pointed image, the image that, in its off-balance, reveals the experience of its chosen theme inviolate from the egoism and questioning of discursive intelligence. Even in Rome he was experimenting with the value of unexpected juxtapositions. In the Parma *Christ Healing the Blind Man* (fig. 8), in a scene of silvery urban grandeur, right beside the main group with its redolent need and solicitude he juxtaposes a foreground figure seen from the back, who points upwards in the opposite direction—no reasons given, no explanation provided. The effect on us of this eloquent and unnecessary figure is catalyst to the whole painting, just like that parallelogram of cloud to the top left in *The Crucifixion*. The recipient of supernatural grace pressed awkwardly against his neighbour's leg is almost lost in the arbitary concerns of his urban group. But this holy and healing act is now seen in its full poignance of inviolable goodness, an act comparable to a mustard seed, and as likely to be lost sight of. It is as daring a 'pointing' of unexpected analogy as we will get at any time in El Greco's career, as unexpected a use of poetic juxtaposition as he would ever muster; but it was not undeliberated. It was a directed intuition of symbolic relationships to outwit the alienating influence of the discursive intellect—a crowning solution to the 'perfection' of Raphael.

When Vitruvius in his treatise *On Architecture* remarks that the architect ought also to be master in other fields such as 'geometry, astrology and music'—so that, presumably, he may pertain to have a full and literate mind—El Greco adds on the margin his own endorsement: 'This manner of going beyond the limits of architecture I find to be the greatest of truths . . . the most illuminating thing he wrote, even if he had written nothing else.' And of course, what El Greco saw here applied to architecture he applied to his own practice of painting. Painting was not a matter of filling in the areas bounded by lines; it was about the new wholes that the literate mind would intuit from the conflicting sciences of a liberal education. Painting, 'because of its universality', stands on the edge of the wide world . . . and 'speculates' till experience can be shared in some more immediate way than the literal description of objects can affect.

The poets at the end of the nineteenth century known as the 'Symbolists' were the first actually to describe the activity of the poetic imagination that El Greco engaged in four hundred years earlier. They had, it should be said, purposes quite different from El Greco—defending the 'inutile' in the age of the machine and pricking the literalism of a bourgeois moral code. Vyacheslav Ivanov, though writing later, gives a typical expression of their view of the action of poetic symbols:

> A symbol is only a true symbol when it is inexhaustible and unlimited in its meaning, when it utters its arcane (hieratic and magical) language of hint and intimation, something that cannot be set forth, that does not correspond to words. It has many faces and many thoughts, and in its remotest depths it remains inscrutable . . . Symbols cannot be stated or explained, and, confronted by their secret meaning in its totality, we are powerless.

From Tintoretto El Greco developed the most far-seeing short circuit of the essential obstacle in the visual language—the alienation of the descriptive and the literal. In El Greco's work the symbol as hieroglyph[3] is destroyed, and then remade from within the experience of its content. The special boon that El Greco was able to offer his own generation was the power of the convinced image: the symbol that has been so reconstituted is, in a sense, 'proved'. This, indeed, we witness in the reactions of modern criticism. As moderns we are all indebted to the artist who so upturns his inherited language as to remove its perennial limitation, and in respect for this achievement his Christianity is acknowledged, even with our 'distance'. The symbols of Christianity as hieroglyphs we have brushed away in our clean-up, but El Greco's remaking of those symbols provide a haunting presence that we are bound to admit.

This was an enterprise fraught with difficulty for El Greco. Throughout his career he kept up the rigour of original creation. Each painting is a new problem; each image is 'pointed' in its own way. In each new painting the device elected to unleash its special energy provides the surprise appropriate for the occasion. Nevertheless, in the Church El Greco enjoyed a profound belonging. Both he and it believed in the mind of the Spirit, and held as common enemy the 'mind of the flesh'. The mind of the literal has always been very much a part of the mind of the flesh, and for a while El Greco was able to hold a standard up to the light of the Church.

The creative leap that El Greco allowed himself to take in Toledo depended on a consensus of religious apperceptions very aptly judged, a perception of high religious culture at a critical moment in history. What El Greco did was inimitable. His son copied his manner, but surely to test his paternal devotion. A studio assistant, Tristan, imitated him marginally more successfully, until he discovered his own robust way of working. It is claimed now that El Greco had pupils, but that he forbade them to paint as he did. This would be reasonable. The proper model for the painter of sacred themes is the iconographic one, in which the sacred narrative is described with an expressive simplicity and purity of style. El Greco's special enterprise enacts a prophetic role as conscience of the reform movement; but, prophet as we may call him, there is still a saving ordinariness about his relationship to the community in which he found himself.

El Greco was fortunate in working in a small city with men who were his intellectual equals, and who were able to appreciate him. But he worked at times in quite humble circumstances, in a studio system for the providing of commodities, to wit, paintings for convents and monasteries. He was a contractor who designed and saw to all the manufacture of huge architectured retables to receive those paintings, retables which were sometimes more costly than the paintings, and he was constantly involved with arbiters who advised him of the payments he should expect to receive. Seeing his work in reproduction we are likely to forget these things. The restless and anxious sentiment in his work has hidden from us the normality of a classic Catholic imagination almost more successfully than if his work had been meretricious. It is just our forgetfulness of the range of that Catholic imagination that has made his work seem so strange to us. To see his work in the London National Gallery, in Munich or New York is to see it out of context. To see it in Toledo is still—even in the last quarter of the twentieth century—to see it in its bed, that strenuous city of high endeavour, the 'New Rome'. It was the city of Lope de Vega, Góngora, Cervantes and St John of the Cross and they all made it together. El Greco was part of a normality.

II

There is a further distortion that history has obtruded on our understanding of El Greco: the value that the last hundred years have placed on mysticism at the expense of the ordinary experience of the Christian. Ever since William James' book, *The Varieties of Religious Experience*, appeared at the end of the nineteenth century, religious experience has been spoken of exclusively in terms of personal feeling and the individual's subjective state.

William James' peculiar prejudice in this matter has become our prejudice, and religious experience is only allowed after a threefold elimination process has taken place. First of all, the social or institutional aspect of religion is politicised and robbed of its symbolic and sacramental nature. If people can be persuaded that the symbols and sacramental system of the Church are, so to speak, man-made, then the institution itself will indeed become an empty husk for them. Without sacraments (the 'visible signs of invisible grace') conferring their hierarchy of effective embodiments, the Church becomes a rule book the rules of which have lost their significance, a town hall as empty as if a revolution had swept through it.

Then having established this primacy of feeling over the social form the intellectual element has to be devalued, for it is only the accretion of a historical tradition. Finally any clear and definite relationship with God has to be eliminated, for to allow that such could be embodied forth in such unreliable things as words would be to admit the call on us of 'dogma', the discredited emission of an empty seat of authority. The result of this critique of William James is to promote, not communion, but exaltation, which he regards as the one true and beneficial element of religion.

Jean Mouroux—lamenting the enthronement in fashion of what is essentially, despite the charm of scientific investigativeness with which William James delivers it, a fundamentalist fallacy to which men have always been prone—argues[4] that, quite to the contrary, religious experience manifests itself as a supremely structured experience. 'It is,' he writes, '. . . the awareness of a

relationship that is known, willed, felt, applied to life, and intro-
duced into human society. More precisely, it is the grasp of a
relationship in which all these elements are integrated into the
simplicity of an act that contains them all virtually, separates
them all from one another as occasion demands, but unifies and
transcends them, because it is the act of a person delivering
himself up to God, who is calling him.'

Finally in one paragraph he relates mystical experience to the
religious experience in a way that, for the headiness of some
responses to El Greco, deserves to be quoted in full.

> But if the mystic is within the faith, if faith is the funda-
> mental principle of both kinds of experience, and if this is
> necessarily so because faith is the axis of the spiritual life,
> we must emphasise the continuity of the two experiences.
> Faith appears in two different states of purity, strength and
> fervour—in one case as a living faith and in the other as a
> lively faith—but in each case the faith is the same, and
> therefore throughout the discontinuity, which may be very
> deeply felt, there must run an extremely profound continuity,
> a radical homogeneity in the aspiration towards God, a
> similarity of life in the two different growths. Therefore
> the mystical life is not a sudden flowering that is foreign to
> the soul (if not an aberration), something absolutely unpre-
> pared for; it cannot even be an experience that follows on
> an absence of experience, appearing as a kind of life
> absolutely new in its principles (the gifts), its objects (God
> as someone seen and felt) and its acts (intuition or experi-
> mental knowledge). On the contrary, it appears as an
> experience that is a continuation of another experience—a
> supreme experience that deepens and purifies, clarifies,
> transcends and crowns a fundamental experience of a more
> humble nature manifesting itself in a diversity of ways. For
> firstly there are already some mystical elements in the
> Christian life—faith, the principle of that life, is a thing that
> involves mysticism and communion from the moment that
> it is born—and secondly, there are moments of ordinary
> Christian life in the genuinely mystical life, because Christian
> behaviour is one, the essential virtues never change, the
> principle and object of faith are the same in both cases, and

(leaving aside, perhaps, the spiritual marriage) mystical experience is neither continuous, nor everlasting, nor unbroken, nor irrevocably separated from the ordinary devout Christian's way of living and loving. Thus in its own interests it is necessary to explain how the mystical experience is, if not inaugurated, at least prepared for by the integral Christian experience—indeed this is the only way of showing that it is not something misleading; and in the interests of Christian experience, it is important to show that this is not something absolutely separate from the mystical experience—otherwise there is the danger of undervaluing the ordinary life of the serious believer and giving undue emphasis to the mystical experience.

I said in Chapter VI that El Greco's language of form is an attempt to hold the distance traversed by God's condescension in a unity that will move us by its urgent relevance for our condition. The human condition as the Christian experiences it can only be described as a betwixt and between, a state that St Bernard described as being between Christ's first and second coming. The Incarnation and the Parousia are the comings of light. Between them are all the comings of grace, the comings and goings of Christ within the soul. This relationship to Christ—in faith—is one which possesses him—though not for itself. But this relationship is also a relationship to Christ who is hoped for and is therefore not possessed: 'the saint is not proud because he hopes in the Lord'. El Greco is the artist of the distance of God, and of the stretch in our soul between our greatness and our misery. The mystic vision does not wipe out that distance or bypass the ordinary graces that are carried by sacraments and the ordinary life of the Church—because they too belong to the same distance.

With El Greco imagination receives its specific Christian task—the transformation of the heart to receive a true manifestation of grace, a true embodiment of the sacred. The soaring figures of his art fill the height and breadth of their pictures because that distance is what must fill the height and breadth of our souls.

So if El Greco is an artist of the 'extraordinary' in the Christian experience this extraordinariness rests upon what was for Toledans in the sixteenth century a profound ordinariness. It was the 'embeddedness' of El Greco's daring perceptions in a normal Catholic sacramentality and imagination that allowed him the intense intellectuality and self-consciousness of his artistic processes. El Greco is the time gatherer of European painting. He holds within his art the points of intersection of all Europe's diverse strands—between the mysticism and the humanism of Catholicism itself, between the historical sense and the sacred, between East and West and between the Middle Ages and Modernity. We notice in him a sensibility that anticipates our own, overwrought, but rigorous—a sensibility that is at once realistic and imagistic. As the English painter, Francis Bacon put it—in our age (which does not have too much time to play with) we are like Alice in Wonderland: we want the smile on the face of the cat, but feel no need to contemplate the whole beast. But when we look at the artists of our own day we find that, brilliant as some of them are, none of them can carry off this interior realism with quite the same conviction as that Greek.

These paintings which are so highly sophisticated, anything, you would say, but innocent, contain at their core the true innocence of wise simplicity. El Greco gathers the heritage of Byzantium, the spirituality of the old iconographers' continuums and submits it with a radiant intelligence to the selfconscious culture of the Renaissance. His radical language of form was created to disturb the expectation of sense, and in the disruption to interpose the divine mystery at the point of the soul's maximum anxiety and capacity for wonder. This programme involved the science of his time but controverted (as Cezanne would have it) in such a way that subsumes it in theology. Because of the rigour of his method we are entitled to call El Greco a philosophical—even a metaphysical—painter. His paintings function at that point of intersection between the spirituality of their content and the consciousness of their programme. Their disturbing power to move is due to the existential way that *caritas* and *gnosis* are allotted such clear respective roles to play in the intuitive task of an imaginative vision.

III

There is good reason to think that the history of art should be taught backwards. No matter how sympathetic the young are to tradition, no art will quite have the vitality to them of what is contemporary: it will be a long time before any old master will have quite the vividness of what is new when you are new. Histories of art are inevitably written the other way round, from the past towards the present. This has meant in Europe that they are histories of an almost inevitable stylistic and technical development marked out by a succession of great names from Giotto to Monet, to be enumerated for their 'discoveries'. It has been too tempting to interpret the arc made by these discoveries as a 'progress', and to ignore what could not be seen to subscribe to it. But artists are concerned with reality as it is present to them, however that may be. They are seldom conscious of developing what the last man did, as if the sequence of style posed a conundrum reaching towards some ultimate solution in the future. What they do they do for themselves, reconciling their vision, their temperament and the science of their craft. If we learn our history of art backwards we discover, not an arc but a web in which thousands of different threads appear, and disappear, and reappear and are lost again, and then, by a contemporary and urgent need, are found yet again. It is salutary to learn the history of art backwards because then we learn the *value* of tradition. To follow art backwards into the past is to follow the pattern of education itself, commencing with our subjective moment in time and our need to secure its objectivity in conflict and brotherhood with all previous generations.

Our acts seem always to have been under a constraint that we did not notice at the time. To go backwards in the history of art is to become aware of the inwardness of creative acts that distinguishes them. The failure of their inwardness will not redeem their brilliance, their worldliness or their rhetoric, once everything is seen for what it is. We find ourselves, involuntarily perhaps, back with Plato's anxiety for the ambiguity offered to the soul in the similitude of representation. It is difficult for the artist to avoid the peculiar sin that Plato allotted to him—to rest in an easy representation. The gravity of world, flesh and self weigh on every decision that the artist makes. To make a decision is sometimes itself the greatest temptation rather that to rest in our unknowing, or await that which contains the proper resonance.

El Greco's sidestep was the most radical gesture of compensation against the ambiguity of similitude favoured in the European tradition; the only time in painting when the Church cast doubt upon the ultimate wisdom of the naturalism that was engulfing it. If El Greco had stayed on Crete, or moved east instead of west he probably would not have been impelled on so radical a direction. Among the scholars residing with El Greco at the Farnese Palace we may surmise some tense dialogues about the Church and the course it might take. The 'classicisers' undoubtedly regarded themselves as an enlightenment, and El Greco would have partially agreed with them—and not agreed with them. He would have seen the Church attacked not only by the Reformers up in Germany and Switzerland, but being sweetly seduced too by the new humanism of the gentlemanly classes. The art of the Church was taken seriously as a language of communication, and here was a whole new breed of scholar artists, the Mannerists, who used their church commissions to show how learned they were. The Church found itself on one hand hosting a dialogue on the Antique, and with the other providing a home for the pyrotechnics of *cadenza* art. El Greco must have taken a few hints from the trouble the Church was having with the Mannerists and decided to seek a new ambiance.

We may assume that the 'New Rome' was a relief to him after the 'Old Rome'. In the New Rome the activity of the Church was more concerted and the pressure of fellow artists less competitive. A profound inspiration as well as a concatenation of circumstances must have sealed the maturity of the early Toledo canvases.

With a superficial sense of history, and no knowledge of the human heart we now equate history with process. Witness possibly of our own irresoluteness, we view every revolution as merely a rehearsal for the next. But such is not what inspires the heart of the flesh and blood reformer. The reformer has his idea set on a certain good and his minimal desire is that his 'good' will be installed independently of what is ill defined as the process and flux of 'life'. There never has been a reform movement in the Church which did not attempt a dismantling of history. El Greco's generation was no exception, and for a while Europe's fate was precariously stilled in the image of eternity. Since the West has bestowed on us the boon of a historical consciousness it is well to be quite frank about what goes on there—in history. There is progress, but there is also loss. Possibly the loss is not noticed; perhaps our attention has been absorbed in some special field where undreamed of progress has taken us by surprise.

Every successive moment of the present offers men a crisis, but man's response to the present is seldom more than half-hearted. It is a patch-up job, and who can blame him if some ingenuity can save the day. Bad habits may deepen to a crisis, and then 'things fall apart, the centre cannot hold.' Suddenly we see through the ingenuity with which we patched things, and the emptiness where should have been a centre catches us by the throat. The splendid artifice crumbles, and a feverish search begins to recover our lost authenticity.

Into the 'to and fro' of history's profit and loss the Church inserts its mysteries. The Church's teaching is the harbinger of origins that remain untouched by history's to and fro. In the Church every man lives out his own history under an eternal typology in a terrifying and yet gracious privacy.

APPENDIX

A SUFI DEFINITION OF IMAGINATION

In respect to my subject I have insisted all along on the two intrinsic realities my contemporaries most anxiously relegate to subjectivity,—the reality of the image as a sort of knowledge (not comparable to discursive knowledge, but parallel to it), and the morally critical intimacy of our response to images in the transactions of artistic taste. A certain ambition to secure the prestige of the image in parity to the word was an abiding preoccupation of the Renaissance from the days of Michelangelo, but El Greco was much too intelligent and sensitive an artist to conceive that parity coming about in illustration. In his search to find the role of imagination in creating the painter's equivalent to 'thought', it may, then, be helpful to consider the theology of a certain Sufi theologian active in the late medieval period, Ibn al'Arabi, who was deeply concerned with imagination.[1]

Like Plotinus before him he saw imagination as an 'in between realm' between spirit and sense. Not being a Platonist he does not use the word 'intellect' in opposition to sense; he uses the theosophical word 'spirit'.

He says: 'Imagination is neither existent nor non-existent, neither known nor unknown, neither affirmed nor denied", and hence he goes on to describe the reality for a man of his image in a mirror. Such a man 'is neither a truth teller nor a liar in his words, "I saw my form, I did not see my form." '

Faced with imagination we are faced with ambiguity, but not merely do we face ambiguity as it applies to our existence; we are faced with it on a cosmic scale. Here Ibn al-'Arabi uses the word 'imagination' interchangeably with 'existence', with everything that is other than the Creator. God is absolute Being. If he is, then his being is incomparably Itself. Since the universe, or what we call 'existence', is that which stands between the absolute being of God, and absolute nothingness, we have to say of it—as we say of imagination—that it exists and that it does not exist. But since the cosmos, while being 'other than God' show us something about God, since God's names and attributes are displayed within it, we can call it the region of God's self-disclosure. Hence, when Ibn al'-Arabi calls the universe 'imagination' he has in view the ambiguous status of all that exists apart from God, and the fact that the universe displays God as in a mirror image—satisfactorily but no more.

For us who are between spiritual and corporeal being the contrast between spirits and bodies is expressed in many pairs of opposites, such as luminous and dark, visible and unseen, inward and outward, high and low, transparent and opaque. In every case imagination is an intermediary reality between the two sides, possessing attributes of both. In imagination everything 'up and down' is known by its attributes. Imagination spiritualises what is corporeal, and embodies what is spiritual.

If God 'discloses' himself to us through similitudes, it is for imagination to 'see' these similitudes and to know 'intuitively' what is seen. Ibn al-'Arabi compared the knowledge we obtained of God in this way to the light of the moon: the rays of the moon are weak and allow us to gaze at it steadily. It is our delight in that special luminosity that allows us so to contemplate her.

The knowledge of God by intellect, the activity of theologians, is compared, on the other hand, to the radiance of the sun which blinds us from what it reveals. Intellect, which is concerned to know God in his essence, is only allowed to find him in his absence. Thus we have here a very complete description of the immanence and transcendence of God, and of the ways in which these two aspects of God are manifest to us. The Muslim theologians placed tremendous emphasis on God's transcendence or 'incomparability', while the Sufis, to which school al-'Arabi belonged, stress equally God's immanence or 'similarity'. Ibn al-'Arabi was concerned to work out a path for the soul in which the visionary and the intellectual will be balanced and brought into helpful relationship. Thus, he writes,

When I entered into this waystation, the self-disclosure in the light without rays fell upon me, so I knew it knowingly. I saw myself through it and saw all things through myself and through the lights which things carry in their essences and which are given them by their realities, not through any extraneous light. I saw a tremendous place of witnessing, in sensory form—not intelligible form—a form of god, not a meaning. In this self-disclosure there became manifest to me the way in which the small expands in order for the large to enter into it, while it remains small and the large remains large, like the camel that passes through the eye of the needle. . . . The small embraces the large, you do not know how, but you do not deny what you see. . .

Through this self-disclosure—which makes the power of the eyes manifest and prefers them over intellects—God made manifest the incapacity of intellects. And through his self-disclosure in radiant light he made manifest the incapacity of eyes and the power of intellects, preferring them over eyes. Thus everything is qualified by incapacity, and God alone possesses the perfection of the Essence.

(Futûhât II, 633)

The dispute in emphasis in Islamic theology between the Muslim and the Sufi schools does not surely seem very remote from the disputes that have occupied the minds of Christian theologians. Anxiety for the defence of the Faith has challenged the intellect to take the initiative and sometimes there has been a tendency for God to be pushed away and away. In our times God has been interiorized to infinitesimal dimensions, while all the time the ancient symbols wherein the 'similitudes' touch the soul have been whittled away by 'explanation'. Our inner life has been left threadbare. By insisting too literally on God's transcendence we have reaped a terrible rebellion in our own immanence which no longer finds the stepping stones in the created world back to its Creator.

El Greco offers, possibly, a balance between the knowledge of God gained in the light of God's (so partial) self-disclosure and the knowledge of God gained by the light that blinds us, the intellectual knowledge of his essence. God's self-disclosure in the world has been disembodied by the artist precisely because his 'incomparability' cannot be embodied. Imagination has edited God's self-disclosure in the world, the better to indicate the incomparability of what can never be disclosed. It is not possible to think of this balance as a compromise, a *via media* between God and Creation, but rather as a mutual reflection (in analogy) between Like and Unlike. El Greco's art acts at the point of interaction on the way where '. . . the small expands in order for the large to enter in to it, while the small remains small and the large remains large.' If we think of the large as being the incomparable aspect of God, and the small as being God's self-disclosure then we have a direct analogy for the function of El Greco's 'disembodiment'. As in Plotinus' spectral light a metamorphosis has happened between things heavenly and things earthly, and '. . . you do not know how, but you do not deny what you see.'

Whether we consider imagination as a microcosm of the combined spiritual and corporeal worlds, or as a specific faculty of the soul, its ultimate significance can only be understood in terms of its relationship to the Divine Reality from which it comes. For imagination to be 'ours' is immediately to subjectify it, to deprive it of its cosmic antipodes in spirit and flesh, and in the end relegate it to the domain of fantasy. Imagination is not God, and it is not us. It is just the gentle agent of our transformation, a way, a pilgrimage, a 'task'.

NOTES

Chapter II
1. See Vladimir Lossky in Leonard Ouspensky and Vladimir Lossky, *The Meaning of Icons* (New York, 1983), p. 69.

Chapter III
1. Jonathan Brown, '*El Greco and Toledo*', in El Greco of Toledo, exhibition catalogue (New York, 1982), p. 83.

Chapter IV
1. See Alonso Perez Sanchez' discussion of this 'probability' in his essay 'On the Reconstruction of El Greco's Dispersed Altarpieces', in *El Greco of Toledo*, op. cit.
2. Richard Mann, *El Greco and his Patrons* (Cambridge, Mass., 1986), p. 80.
3. Op. cit., pp. 100f.
4. The retable is known to have been dispersed within a generation of El Greco's death.
5. Coll. Museo Balaguer; presently on loan to the Prado.

Chapter V
1. See Fritzjof Schuon, *Logic and Transcendence*, p.17
2. Significantly it was on Raphael's example academies were founded.
3. *Sculpting in Time* (London, 1986), pp. 48f.

Chapter VI
1. See Chapter III, discussion of the Prado *Crucifixion*.
2. Rudolf Wittkower, 'El Greco's Language of Gesture', in his *Allegory and the Migration of Symbols* (New York, 1987).
3. *Enneads* IV, 3.
4. See John Dillon's essay, 'Plotinus and the Transcendental Imagination' in *Religious Imagination*, ed. J.P. Mackey (Edinburgh 1986).

5. *De Mysteriis* III, 14.
6. See *El Greco and his Patrons*, op. cit., p. 137.
7. See John Dillon, art. cit.
8. *Enneads* VI, 4.
9. See Appendix, 'A Sufi Definition of Imagination', p.104ff.
10. Preface to *Thoughts for Meditation: A Way to Recovery from Within*, selected and arranged by N. Gaugulee (London, 1951), p.12.

Chapter VIII
1. The ubiquitous invention of photo reproduction and André Malraux.
2. Probably the third canvas painted for the top tier of the retable at the College of the Incarnation.
3. A 'hieroglyph' is an image meant to be read with a set meaning.
4. See his *The Christian Experience* (London, 1955), pp. 16 and 45-46.

Appendix
1. W. Chittick, Imagination and Imagery in Ibn al-'Arabi, *Temenos* 10 (London, 1989), p. 99.

BIBLIOGRAPHY

Jonathan Brown, 'El Greco and Toledo' and A.E. Perez Sanchez, 'On the reconstruction of El Greco's dispersed altarpieces' in *El Greco of Toledo*, exhibition catalogue (New York, 1982).

William Chittick, 'Imagination & Poetic Imagery according to Ibn al-'Arabi' in *Temenos*, Arts Review (London, 1989).

John Dillon, 'Plotinus and the Transcendental Imagination', in *Religious Imagination*, ed. J.P. Mackey (Edinburgh, 1986).

Jose Gudiol, *El Greco* (London, 1973).

Richard Mann, *El Greco and his Patrons*, monograph in Cambridge Studies in the History of Art (Cambridge, Mass., 1986)

Jean Mouroux, *The Christian Experience*, (London, 1955).

Lionello Puppi, *El Greco* (London, 1968).

Leonard Ouspensky with Vladimir Lossky, *The Meaning of Icons* (New York, 1983).

Andrew Tarkowsky, *Sculpting in Time* (London, 1986).

Rudolf Wittkower, chapter on 'El Greco's Language of Gesture' in his *Allegory and the Migration of Symbols* (New York, 1987).